M000084525

Who Needs
a Friend
When You Can Make
a Disciple?

Who Needs a Friend When You Can Make a Disciple?

Two Women's Journey to Biblical Friendship

Barbara Enter & Gina Weinmann

As Christians, we are to help one another become as much like the Lord Jesus Christ as possible. That is what Barbara and Gina have shown us in their very personal journey to a sweet, biblical friendship. Their stories keep your interest and the Scriptures are right on target for the discipleship topic. Another big plus is their insightful questions at the end of every chapter, which are perfect for individual or group study. I am glad to recommend this book to you.
MARTHA PEACE: ACBC counselor and author of *The Excellent Wife*

What better way to delve into the particulars of biblical discipleship than to read this poignant account of how two women took that journey together—one the discipler and the other the disciplee. You will see how Jesus Christ is their life and that growing into His likeness is their goal. You will see them searching God's Word as their source of hope, guidance, comfort, and for all they need to face life, even cancer. Sometimes life is messy and hard, and you will see them model transparency as they share weaknesses and are the kind of friends we need that will ask hard questions and hold us accountable. They show you how you will not only have made a disciple but a lifelong friend who will be faithful to the end.
MARY SOMERVILLE, MA Pastoral Counseling: Adjunct Faculty, The Master's University, Santa Clarita, CA

I am thankful that Barbara and Gina have written this beautiful testimony to the blessings of in-depth discipleship relationships. I, too, have experienced the blessing of friendships that come out of mentoring others to follow the Lord. I was also reminded of the beauty of knowing and using Scripture to help others navigate the whitewater of life. Barbara and Gina have been through a lot together as they have followed the Lord. Praise the Lord that they have Him as their guide and goal, Scripture as the source of wisdom, and one another as friends on the journey. Your friendships will be deeper and richer by following their advice and example, by focusing on discipleship relationships not just friendship relationships.
ERNIE BAKER: Pastor of Counseling of First Baptist Church of Jacksonville and Chairman of the online Bachelor's degree in Biblical Counseling at The Master's University. Author of *Marry Wisely, Marry Well; Help! I'm in a Conflict* and *Help! Disability Pressures Our Marriage.*

Christian relationships in the church today are driven more by cultural custom and practice than by biblical truth. There is an acceptable veneer of superficiality to most relationships because the fear of man overrules the fear of God. Sometimes that involves one Christian's fear of confronting another because he or she does not want to be labeled as "judgmental"! Sometimes there is the fear of being too vulnerable, revealing besetting sins, and losing that less-than-perfect image! True biblical friendship is not afraid of either because it is rooted in the rich dynamic of discipleship. What Barbara Enter and Gina Weinmann have written in *Who Needs a Friend When You Can Make a Disciple? Two Women's Journey to Biblical Friendship* is a powerful challenge to the wrong notions of real biblical relationships. Their robust experience in counseling and teaching women in the church provides the right practical backdrop to illustrate their goal, and provides a road map for meaningful change. If a Christian woman is going to make the necessary changes in her relationships, she must be intentional and driven by the ultimate motivation to bring her Lord great glory! Then this book is a must read!

DR. JOHN D. STREET: Chair, BC Graduate Program, The Master's University & Seminary; President, Association of Certified Biblical Counselors Board of Trustees

I think this book will be very helpful in drawing the connection between biblical counseling and discipleship. Many people, even Christians, don't understand that counseling is a form of fulfilling the last command Christ gave to us as His disciples in Matthew 28:18–20 before ascending to the right hand of the Father. It was the command to go and make disciples. Here we have what is called The Great Commission that has become for many Christians "The Great Omission." It is my considered opinion after being in what is sometimes called full-time Christian Service as an elder/pastor and trainer of Christians for service in the church for sixty-three years that Christians may know that they are to be disciple makers, but they don't know how to do it. This book will take the mystery out of making disciples and help Christians to know how to change this last command of Jesus from being a great omission to fulfilling it as The Great Commission. I recommend it highly for that purpose.

DR. WAYNE MACK: Pastor/elder of counseling at Lynnwood Baptist Church in Pretoria, South Africa; Missionary sent out by Grace Missions International, the missionary arm of Grace Community Church in California

Who Needs a Friend When You Can Make a Disciple?
Two Women's Journey to Biblical Friendship

Copyright © 2020 Shepherd Press

ISBNS:
978-1-63342-219-3 paper
978-1-63342-220-9 epub
978-1-63342-221-6 mobi

Unless noted otherwise, Scripture quotations are taken from the New American Standard Bible® (NASB), Copyright © 1960, 1962, 1963, 1968, 1971, 1972, 1973, 1975, 1977, 1995 by The Lockman Foundation.
Used by permission. www.Lockman.org

No part of this publication may be reproduced, or stored in a retrieval system, or transmitted, in any form or by any means, mechanical, electronic, photocopying, recording or otherwise, without the prior permission of Shepherd Press.

Cover design and typeset by www.greatwriting.org

Printed in the United States of America

Shepherd Press
P.O. Box 24
Wapwallopen, PA 18660
www.shepherdpress.com

Contents

Dedications

....

Barbara dedicates this book to

Dr. Wayne A. Mack, a God-fearing man who taught me how to
start closing the gap between my formal theology and my functional
theology through his biblical teaching
on the doctrine of the Sufficiency of Scripture.
You, my spiritual father, are a gift from my Heavenly Father.

❖

Gina dedicates this book to

Lauren, my daughter and sister in the faith.
May you both be and find a "Gina."

❖

I thank my God in all my remembrance of you . . .
because I have you in my heart . . .
(Philippians 1:3, 7b)

Acknowledgments

Proverbs 27:2 states, "Let another praise you, And not your own mouth; A stranger, and not your own lips." As such, we wholeheartedly wish to thank those involved with helping us bring this book to fruition. First, we would like to thank all those at Shepherd Press, particularly Jim and Sue Holmes, for guiding us through this process. They have made this endeavor enjoyable with their guidance and expertise. Anything lacking in this volume is due only to our limitations, not theirs.

A huge thank you as well to all who read the early manuscript and gave pointers and suggestions along the way. Your input in the initial stages of our writing helped us solidify both the format and the content of our book.

We would also like to thank those who have been instrumental in shepherding and teaching us over the years, in particular Pastors Alan Wilson, David Bailey, and Ty Blackburn. The Lord has been extremely kind in giving us such faithful men who hold to a high view of Scripture.

Most importantly, an affectionate thanks to our husbands, Jack and Craig, for always encouraging us to use our spiritual gifts and for giving us the time to minister to others. Without their love and support, we would certainly not have had the time to write our book.

And finally, but mostly importantly, the highest praise and thanks goes to our great God and Savior, Jesus Christ. He brought us to Himself and then knit our hearts together in Him. We "are looking for the blessed hope and the appearing of the glory of our great God and Savior, Christ Jesus, who gave Himself for us to redeem us . . ." (Titus 2:13-14a). We cannot wait to see HIM!

Foreword

DR. WAYNE MACK

*Pastor/Elder of Lynnwood Baptist Church in Pretoria, South Africa;
Professor of Biblical Counseling at Strengthening Ministries
Training Institute; Member of Academy of the Association of
Certified Biblical Counselors; Director of Association of Certified
Biblical Counselors in Africa; Author of numerous books on Biblical
Counseling and Christian Living Subjects; Past Chairman and
Developer of the Master of Arts in Biblical Counseling Program at
the Master's University*

The title of this book, *Who Needs a Friend When You Can Make a Disciple?*, is an intriguing title to a very helpful book. In evangelical circles we often hear a lot about discipleship, but seldom hear or read about the specifics of how to actually do the work of discipling. In this book, Barbara and Gina bring the ministry of discipleship down to the "nuts" and "bolts" of what it looks like in actual practice. Though the contents of this book are based squarely on biblical principles, the outworking of those principles is described in extremely personal and understandable and repeatable ways.

After more than fifty years in ministry while working with thousands of people, my observation is that many Christians know they should be involved in "making disciples." And, it seems to me that most Christians actually want to obey the Lord's clear command in Matthew 28:19. Yet, for many of them, the Great Commission still remains the great omission. After many years of being a Christian, they still cannot point to one person whom they have brought to Christ or specifically helped to grow into Christlikeness. In my opinion, what many of these people seem to need is practical and relevant instruction on the "how to" aspects of "making disciples." In writing this book, Barb and Gina have taken this ministry out of the clouds where doing the work of discipling seemed above and beyond what many average Christians can do. Through their personal experience, based on a robust knowledge of Scripture, they have provided the very "how to," down-to-earth, repeatable instructions that Christians may need to actually do what Christ commanded. Reading the contents of each chapter and completing the application questions at the end of each chapter make this book a valuable means of discipling people to do the work of discipling.

If, in picking up this book, you were looking for a major catalyst for you in your service to Christ in being the disciple and discipler that He wants every Christian to be, this book should be of great assistance to you in that endeavor. If you read and heed the contents of this book, I have no doubt that you will be personally strengthened and enriched in your own life and in your outreach to others for His sake.

Preface

When we tell people the title of our book, we sure do get some strong reactions! Our intention is certainly not to downplay friendships or even usurp the priority of the marital relationship. Rather, we want to show ladies that through the process of discipleship they can find a faithful friend. This is what happened to us.

We have observed more often than not, when women come to a new church, they seem to be on an endless search to "find a friend" so they can "feel" a part or "feel" connected. As Christian women, we often go about finding a friend in the *wrong manner*. Based on common interests or a similar "season of life," we seek out that one special friend at church. We look for someone who will help us "feel a sense of belonging." While that is not wrong, there is a better way to find that special "friend," the friend who sticks closer to you than a brother (Prov. 18:24).

We think a better way—in fact, a more biblical way—would be for women to come into a church with the solid knowledge that they are a part of the body of Christ and, therefore, with the intention that they would do their part in serving the body of Christ. As a result, they will most assuredly "feel a part." We often tell young women, "You *are a part*; so, *do your part* and then you will *feel a part*." A part of your "part" within the church is developing discipleship relationships. A discipleship relationship between an older woman and a younger woman is vital for spiritual growth (Titus 2:3–5). It saddens us to see the lack of such relationships among women in the church, especially as we reflect on the rich blessings of God on our own discipleship journey.

That's why we're writing this book! We want other women to find a faithful friend through the process of discipleship.

We had talked about writing a book for a long time, but we became serious about writing as a result of two events. First, we were discipling two young women who had requested help with their relationship as it had recently undergone quite a change. As we talked with them, we suddenly realized that very few women enjoy a discipleship relationship like God has graciously granted to us. Helping these women to think biblically about what they were experiencing, presented us with some opportunities to reflect in practical ways on our own relationship. We realized that, while we didn't take our relationship for granted, what we did assume was that other women both had and enjoyed the blessings of the kind of relationship we shared. How wrong we were!

One day while meeting with these two women, I (Barbara) distinctly remember Gina looking at me and saying, "I guess we are best friends!" We had never regarded our relationship in that way and had never articulated the obvious. We had always considered our relationship as one of discipleship since I am almost twenty years older than Gina. However, on that particular day, we finally realized our discipleship relationship had become a cherished friendship.

The second catalyst that got us started writing this book was cancer. Gina was diagnosed with a rare type of bone marrow cancer. By the time she got to the doctor for treatment, she was gravely ill, needing blood and platelet transfusions as well as chemotherapy. Cancer provided Gina an opportunity to consider what she really wanted to accomplish despite her illness. Writing this book was one of those goals. We decided the time had come to write this book when Gina stated that if she died, her one regret would be that we had not written our story. In fact, we wrote the thesis of this book and the chapter titles when Gina was hooked up to IVs, getting a blood transfusion! What else is there to do for six hours?

Gina went into remission through her treatment plan, but her cancer returned after four years. She underwent treatment a second time, followed by an autologous stem cell transplant in the hopes of securing a longer remission. Although we had written a rough draft of our book before her transplant, it was during her recovery period that we made our final edits. Gina did not get the longer remission her family and doctors were hoping for. In fact, what was supposed to have been about a five-year remission from the stem cell transplant turned into only sixteen months. We are thankful Gina is currently in remission again, taking a daily "chemo" pill.

Why should you listen to us, though? Gina has a BSE in Secondary Education in English and I graduated from The Master's College (now University) with a Master of Arts in Biblical Counseling. We both are certified through The Association of

Certified Biblical Counselors, ACBC (previously known as NANC). Also, we are actively involved in the counseling and discipleship ministry of our church, Providence Church in Duluth, Georgia.

However, our degrees and certifications don't qualify us to write a book on discipleship. What qualifies us is the fact that God, in His providence, forged a deep friendship between us through the process of discipleship. Our relationship, built around His Word and sustained by His grace, has taught us much and strengthened us both as we seek to be disciples of Jesus Christ.

One of the first things we discuss in this book is how we came to know Christ and what drew us together on our joint road of discipleship. In doing so, we define discipleship and point out what *DID NOT* draw us together—you may be surprised! Next, we highlight some practical "how tos" to help you implement biblical ways to practice and sustain discipleship with the women around you. Many of these "how tos" have their basis in various one-anothering passages. We have also interspersed biblical instruction throughout the chapters. This instruction has helped us to obey the Great Commission of Jesus, recorded in Matthew 28:19–20: "Go therefore and make disciples of all the nations, baptizing them in the name of the Father and the Son and the Holy Spirit, teaching them to observe all that I commanded you; and lo, I am with you always, even to the end of the age."

In the process, you will be reminded that our Lord said to "make disciples"; but He never said "go and make friends!" If we are not careful, church can be reduced to a mere social club.

Ultimately, we long for our sisters in Christ to understand the importance of true biblical discipleship and to be equipped to put feet and hands to their understanding. This book is written to encourage women to stop looking for that *special* friend and to start discipling other women in order to find that *faithful* friend. Through sharing our personal story, it is our prayer that you'll see the impact discipleship can have on your spiritual growth as it has had on ours. Moreover, we pray that you will gain a deeper understanding of the role that discipleship plays in our efforts to "stimulate one another to love and good deeds" (Heb. 10:24).

1

The Journey Begins

And He said to them,
"Follow Me, and I will make you fishers of men."
(Matthew 4:19)

• • • • • • • • • • •

Have you ever gone to an event with other people, enjoyed the event immensely, but come away remembering something totally different than they did? For example, at a circus, one spectator may be focused on the clowns that are coming into the arena while another spectator may focus on the dogs doing their tricks on another part of the floor. Gina and my memories of how our relationship began are like the two spectators. We both agree the relationship began; that's pretty obvious. But the focus on what was important to each of us in how the relationship began is quite different. However, since our relationship is based on another foundational relationship, I (Barbara) would like to tell you about my relationship with Jesus Christ and when I became His disciple.

Becoming a Disciple of Jesus Christ

I was born in Atlanta, Georgia, the youngest of six children. I was raised in that area my whole life, surrounded by extended family, with my siblings and cousins being some of my best friends. My home life was one of pleasant memories. My parents were strong, godly Christians, who displayed the fruit of the Spirit consistently before me. For many years, I assumed that my home life was very much the normal experience. Sadly, as an adult, I discovered that my family was in many ways "abnormal," since we were so close and enjoyed one another immensely.

Despite my wonderful Christian upbringing, it was not until I went off to Georgia Southern College (now Georgia Southern University) that I came to know the Lord. Until that point in my life, I thought I was a good person. I was not involved in any "sinful" activities, or so I thought. At college, I started smoking, drinking, and trying "to discover who I was." However, I did not like who I was becoming. So, I thought I would try to become more religious by reading my Bible. I started in Matthew and found the Bible to be terribly boring and beyond my understanding. Finally, I came to the point of hating who I had become. It was then that I contemplated suicide. Instead of taking my life, however, I can remember standing in my dorm room and crying out to God one evening: "God if you are real, you will have to show me because I just don't believe you are real." God answered that prayer on Friday, February 13, 1970 around 8:30 p.m. at a meeting which was designed to teach Christians how to share their faith. In a meeting held in one of the lecture rooms, I met the living God through His Son, Jesus Christ.

I went to that meeting sponsored by Campus Crusade for Christ in order to learn how to share my faith because I thought I was a believer. (Plus, it didn't hurt that a guy I liked was going to the meeting!) It never occurred to me to doubt that I was a Christian because I was raised in a Christian home. So, surely, I was a believer. As far as I can remember, I always believed in a God. I also believed that Jesus died for my sins and He died for my sins because I was such a good person. Herein was the problem! My thinking did not line up with the biblical gospel. At the meeting on that Friday, I learned that ". . . there is none righteous, not even one; there is none who understands, there is none who seeks for God; all have turned aside, together they have become useless; there is none who does good, there is not even one" (Rom. 3:10–12). Jesus did not die for me because I was a good person; He died for me because I was *not* a good person. Furthermore, the lady who was leading the meeting told me that although I was a sinner, I could be saved by grace. I learned that evening that it is by ". . . grace you have been saved through faith; and that not of yourselves, it is the gift of God; not as a result of works, so that no one may boast" (Eph. 2:8–9). I could not earn my salvation by being a good person or by doing good works, which amounts to filthy rags in God's sight (Isa. 64:6). However, I could be saved by grace through faith. The leader of the meeting continued to instruct me that evening. The verse that God used to shine the light of the gospel into my darkened heart was from the book of Romans: "But God demonstrates His own love toward us, in that while we were yet sinners, Christ died for us" (5:8). When I heard that verse read, I knew it was *the truth*—Christ died for me while I was yet a sinner, not while I was a good person!

I have always found it interesting that my conversion was so unemotional. At that time of my life, being a young lady, I was very emotional. However, when I heard the truth of the gospel, I thought to myself, "What this lady is saying is *the truth*." "I just heard *the truth*." There were no emotions, but I knew I was hearing the true gospel, not one of my own imagination. I repented of my sins that evening, and I placed my faith solely in Jesus Christ. No longer did I trust in my own self-righteousness, but I was trusting in the righteousness of Jesus Christ and His sacrificial atoning death. I walked home from the meeting knowing that the guilt of my sin was gone. I had met Jesus Christ who once said, ". . . I am the way, and the truth, and the life; no one comes to the Father but through Me" (John 14:6). Jesus had reconciled me to God and He was the door through which I went to meet God, my Heavenly Father. I had become a new creation (2 Cor. 5:17).

As a new creation, I realized that I was now an ambassador for Christ. Second Corinthians 5:20 says, "Therefore, we are ambassadors for Christ, as though God were making an appeal through us; we beg you on behalf of Christ, be reconciled to God." I had a new reason for living and I had a new mission. That new mission involved making disciples of Jesus Christ.

I have known my Lord since that day in February, 1970. My desire has been to "proclaim Him, admonishing every man [woman] and teaching every man [woman] with all wisdom, so that we [I] may present every man [woman] complete in Christ. For this purpose also I labor, striving according to His power, which mightily works within me" (Col. 1:28–29). I also desire to be a Titus 2 woman who teaches younger women to love God and to love others so that the Word of God will not be dishonored (Titus 2:3–5). I have had the high privilege of discipling many women as I have walked with the Lord. Gina is one of those special ladies.

My first memories of Gina are of her sitting in a Bible study that I was teaching at our former church, Grace Bible Church, a church my husband, Jack, and I helped to start with a handful of other believers in 1978. Gina and her husband, Craig, began attending Grace in January 1994. Gina was newly married and obviously a young believer. As I was teaching the classes, Gina was always full of questions (and I do mean full and overflowing)! On one particular day, while we were standing in the kitchen of the church, Gina was talking about her life before coming to the Lord. Her life obviously involved some sin, as is true for all people—sins she had committed and sins committed against her (Rom. 3:23). She had been told that it would take her a long time to get over her past. In effect, she was told that she would never get "past" her past. This unbiblical counsel was robbing Gina of hope. It grieved me to see how her unbiblical thinking was affecting her, as all unbiblical thinking does. I realized at that point that Gina could use some intentional, one-on-one discipleship in order to help her think biblically about her past.[1]

I wanted Gina to know the truth so the truth could set her free from her past (John 8:32). Gina was made a new creation when she came to know the Lord. As such, she did not need to be shackled to her past or remain a victim of it any longer. She could learn to think and respond biblically to her past, and I wanted to teach her how to do just that. I wanted to teach her because of the pain she was experiencing. My heart went out to her out of compassion. I wanted to come alongside of her as she walked with the Lord and speak the truth to her in love so she could mature in Christ (Eph. 4:15). While we did not start meeting formally, I felt compelled to start teaching her how to think biblically about her past.

In listening to Gina that day in the church kitchen, I knew that standing before me was a young lady who needed help. She needed help in the form of discipleship. My heart was moved toward her due to this need, not due to any other reason. It was not her personality that drew me to her. It was not our commonality that drew us together. What drew me to her was recognizing a spiritual need in a young believer. Consequently, we had many informal conversations about what it means to be a new creation and to be united to Christ. This instruction went along with the teaching she received from the pulpit and in Bible studies.

To help Gina get "past" her past, I began to teach her the spiritual reality of how her old "self" was dead and how her old "man" had been crucified (Eph. 4:22; Col. 3:9; Rom. 6:6). She began

---

1   We highly recommend Stephen Viars' excellent book *Putting Your Past In Its Place* (Eugene, OR: Harvest House Publishers, 2011).

to understand that she had a new "self" and a new heart with new desires (Jer. 32:38–40; Ezek. 36:26–29). She had been baptized into Christ and now she needed to learn how to live accordingly (Rom. 6:3). I was able to teach Gina what it meant to be immersed into Jesus Christ. Kenneth S. Wuest explains the concept of being baptized into Christ as an "introduction or placing of a person or thing into a new environment or into union with something else so as to alter its condition or its relationship to its previous environment or condition."[2] Gina could put her past in the past because she was now a different person, a new person living in a new environment. Her condition had been permanently altered!

Gina began to learn that although her past does impact her, it does not define who she is now that she is united to Christ. Some people teach that a person's past is nothing. This unbiblical view minimizes the pain people experience from being sinned against and also minimizes the sin that people commit against others. On the other hand, some people wrongly teach that a person's past is everything. For instance, I have counseled women who have been told that their past is "everything" and this is what is causing their present behavior. I have even talked to seventy-year-old women who are still "stuck" in their past. They blame their "past" for their worry, fear, and anxiety. They live as if they are still victims of their past. The view that one's past is nothing as well as the view that one's past is everything harms people. The Bible, on the other hand, teaches us that we are not victims. Indeed, it teaches us that we can overwhelmingly be conquerors through Christ who loves us (Rom. 8:37). It saddens me to see women who are "stuck" in their past due to unbiblical teaching and thinking. I wanted more for Gina, so I kept instructing her.

I taught Gina, too, that our past is not ultimately what causes our behavior, although it does influence us. We all develop what the Bible calls a "manner of life" (Eph. 4:22). A manner of life is simply the habits that we have developed through the years. We decide at an early age how we are going to respond to life, how we are going to respond to others, how we are going to respond to conflicts, etc. Outside of Christ, all of our habitual patterns are ungodly. However, when we are united to Christ, we can start

---

2   As quoted by John MacArthur, Jr., *The MacArthur New Testament Commentary: Romans 1–8* (Chicago, IL: Moody Press, 1991), 320.

putting off our ungodly "manner of life" and putting on a godly "manner of life" one step at a time. One man describes it this way: We all have ungodly "ruts." Yet we can start making godly "ruts," as we learn to walk in a manner that pleases God (Eph. 4:1). As a believer, Gina came to understand that she could change and not be imprisoned by her past.

Furthermore, Gina came to understand that no one remembers his or her past 100 percent correctly. We often interact and interpret past events in creative ways. Let me illustrate this with a funny story. My brother once asked my mother why she made him take ballet. Mom chuckled and informed him that he certainly did not take ballet but did ride with her once to pick up my sister from ballet class. However, in my brother's memories, he had been forced to take ballet! To further illustrate my point, I was teaching a class this principle using this personal story when I casually mentioned to the class that my family went to Jekyll Island for vacation every summer. My sister, who was in the class, gave a hearty laugh and informed me and the class that we only went to Jekyll Island one summer, not every summer. So, you see, memories cannot be relied upon to give valid information.

Moreover, our memories are most of the time self-favoring. Proverbs 16:2 says, "All the ways of a man are clean in his own sight, But the LORD weighs the motives." In other words, we tend to remember our part in our past as "clean" or "innocent." Many times we are innocent, but often we respond to events in a sinful manner. This tendency to favor self can be seen when people tell in vivid details what others have done to them. When they are asked how they responded, they quickly quip, "I don't remember" or "I didn't do anything or say anything." Their memories are too self-favoring to remember that they responded in an unkind way.

One more important principle with which Gina had to come to grips is the truth that God is sovereign over her past. Romans 8:28 is such an encouraging reminder that ". . . God causes all things to work together for good to those who love God, to those who are called according to His purpose." Gina came to know this truth and appreciate it. She quickly got "past" her past, as she allowed me to minister God's Word to her. Thus, our joint journey began.

For Further Thought

....

1. Consider conversations you have had with women at church in the last few weeks. Is there a person that you can identify who needs some help thinking biblically about a circumstance, a situation, or an event? How can you intentionally minister the Word to her?

2. Gina's spiritual need involved dealing biblically with her past. If this is a spiritual need of yours or someone you know, would you consider going through Stephen Viars' book *Putting Your Past in Its Place* together with another woman?

3. Did you notice, in Gina's story, that she did not recognize her spiritual need? Her lack of recognition shows us the urgent need for discipleship.

4. In this chapter, Barbara has shared her testimony of how she came to know Christ. Is there a woman with whom you can share your testimony over a cup of coffee?

5. All of our spiritual blessings flow from our union with Christ. Read Ephesians 1 and make a list of all that is true because you are in Christ. Now spend some time in worship and adoration for such a marvelous Savior!

6. Is there an older woman whom you could approach with a request for her to disciple you in a certain area?

2

Gina Joins the Journey

Two are better than one because they have a good return for their labor. For if either of them falls, the one will lift up his companion. But woe to the one who falls when there is not another to lift him up.
(Ecclesiastes 4:9–10)

• • • • • • • • • • • • •

Most of us have seen the commercial of an older lady falling and she cries out, "Help! I've fallen and I can't get up!" Of course, a loved one finally rescues the elderly person and there is a device advertised that will prevent this dangerous situation from happening again. All the victim has to do, if she falls again, is push a button on her necklace and professional help will come. While this commercial can become rather annoying after watching it numerous times, the truth remains that if you fall, it is comforting to have a loved one present to help you get up. The discipleship relationship can bring such comfort.

Gina Becomes a Disciple of Jesus Christ

I (Gina) am originally from the Bronx, New York. My birth mother died of aplastic anemia when I was two years old. My father eventually remarried after we moved to Georgia in 1973. My brother and I didn't have lots of family or cousins around due to distance but we spent summers in New York with my grandparents. It was during these times up North that I heard all the family stories about the old country, Italy, and grew to appreciate good food. You probably can guess that I was born into a Roman Catholic family. We only went to church at Easter and Christmas, but we kids were made to attend catechism school. In high school, I announced to my parents that I no longer wanted to attend church. I actually told them that they couldn't make me go since they never went themselves. They didn't have a leg to stand on. Thus, began the time in my life that reminds me of the theme of the book of Judges: ". . . every man did what was right in his own eyes" (Judg. 17:6). I truly had no fear of God before my eyes (Ps. 36:1).

Unlike Barbara, I have no recollection of the exact time or date when I was converted. I remember hearing the gospel for the first time from a Baptist youth pastor the summer after high school graduation. I prayed the "sinner's prayer," walked the aisle, and was baptized. I now understand the emptiness of what is often called "easy believism," which is what I was participating in that day. Easy believism is a view that states that a person only has to pray a prayer or walk down an aisle of a church to receive salvation but does not have to bear any godly fruit in his or her life. This view is in opposition to the parable that Jesus taught in Matthew 13. Indeed, it is a false gospel.

Looking back, I now realize that I was the rocky soil and not the good soil (Matt. 13:1–23). In other words, I was not truly born again that day because I was not the good soil which is described in Matthew 13:23: "And the one on whom seed was sown on the good soil, this is the man who hears the word and understands it; who indeed bears fruit and brings forth, some a hundredfold, some sixty, and some thirty."

I know this because I quickly reverted to my sinful lifestyle, only now I felt guilty for the way I was living. I reasoned that Jesus was indeed the Savior but not for someone as sinful as I was. Thinking that the gospel was out of reach for me, I wavered between hopelessness and anger.

At various times, I was exposed to the gospel over the course of the next several years. One of those times was when Craig shared his testimony with me on one of our first dates. I knew what he was telling me was the truth. I would have called myself a believer at that point. However, it was only after my marriage to Craig in 1992 and after we began attending the church to which Barbara and Jack belonged that I was truly born again and started to grow spiritually. Like many Christians, I have no remembrance of the exact moment of my salvation. Nonetheless, as I sit here typing today, I have assurance of my salvation for many reasons. First, God has caused me to persevere for many years, even through the severe trial of cancer. Second, the Holy Spirit Himself bears witness to my spirit that I am a child of God (Rom. 8:16).

Even though I was finally growing spiritually at our new church, I seemed stuck in my past. I kept rehearsing all that I had done as well as what had been done to me before my conversion. I couldn't make it through a hymn at church without sobbing. I wasn't touched primarily by the truth of the greatness of God or the kindness of our Savior expressed in the song, but because whatever we sang always became in my mind all about me, my feelings, my past, and my story.

Barbara and I initially got to know each other through my attendance at the women's Bible studies she led. While Barbara remembers a kitchen conversation we had about my past, I truly don't. I'd love to use the excuse of time or even "chemo brain." If I'm honest, however, it's more likely because of how self-focused I was at that point in my life. What I do remember is that, eventually, I started opening up to Barbara and telling her about my past. I thought if I could tell Barbara about every sin I could remember committing, I would "get over" my past. She responded by saying that there was no need for me to confess every sin to her. She also explained that there was no need to review them because the Lord took no remembrance of them (Jer. 31:34). She told me that when God looks at me, He sees me in Christ, as having lived Christ's perfect life.

Over time, I learned to stop rehearsing my former sins whenever they came to mind. Whenever I caught myself going through the list, no matter where I was in the list, I would stop and recall that each sin had been forgiven, paid for by Christ's atoning sacrifice on my behalf because I believed on Him. He who knew no sin became sin for me so that I might become the righteousness of God in Christ (2 Cor. 5:21). What a great exchange! To know that our salvation and even our current standing before God is all of His mercy and grace—not dependent upon our behavior—brings freedom to obey Him out of a heart of gratitude and love rather than compulsion.

Little did I know how the Lord would use Barbara to teach me not just how to get past my past, but also about love, kindness, and friendship. Little did I know how much she and I would come to love each other and experience true biblical fellowship. I do think it is very important to remember there is a distinction between what the Bible calls fellowship and what our Christian culture calls fellowship. In our churches, most of us refer to social times together as fellowship. We may go out to lunch with a friend for some "fellowship" or attend a party for some "fellowship." Although social times together can be beneficial, this is not what the Bible calls fellowship.

In our Bibles, the word that is translated fellowship comes from the Greek word *koinonia*, which is rich "fellowship with, participation in . . . a communion . . ."[3] When Paul writes to the believers in Philippi, he tells them how he remembers them in prayer with much joy because of their "participation in the gospel" (Phil. 1:5). The word used here for participation is *koinonia*. In other words, there is richness in their fellowship because of their joint participation, their joint sharing in spreading the good news of Jesus Christ.

Consider Paul and Timothy's relationship. They were initially drawn together due to true *koinonia*, this joint participation in spreading the gospel. It was not because of similar backgrounds, a common career, or being in the same season of life. Rather, they were drawn together as they ministered the gospel to the church in Philippi (Acts 16). This is the type of fellowship that God has so graciously allowed Barbara and me to experience.

The Discipleship Relationship Becomes Cemented

Most of us have heard the old adage: "The Lord works in mysterious ways." Without going into a dissertation on God's providence, Barbara and I have found that He usually works through ordinary means. God did not zap us one day and suddenly we were BFFs. Instead, He used a sobering event to bring us closer than we were previously, thus cementing our relationship.

This event occurred when I was weaning myself from antidepressant drugs in 2000. Let me explain. At the time my second child, Andrew, was born, Craig drove a delivery truck. Sleep was a high priority for Craig so I took Andrew downstairs for nighttime feedings. I watched Nick at Night while nursing him. To say

3   Spiros Zodhiates, Th.D., *The Hebrew-Greek Key Study Bible* (Chattanooga, TN: AMG Publishers, 1990), 1848.

watching TV was a huge mistake is an understatement! At first, I only watched a few shows: Dick Van Dyke and That Girl; but soon, I was watching TV half the night, only going to bed when Craig left for work by 5:30 a.m., or so. Obviously, I was not getting adequate sleep. By the time Andrew was one year old, I was not functioning well, sleeping about three hours a night. The sleep deprivation caused by my own poor choices brought on a depression.

With Craig's support, Barbara and two other friends from church came over one evening to discuss a plan to help me. Against Barbara's judgment, I went on antidepressants and sleeping pills which were prescribed by my primary care physician (interestingly, my OB/GYN wouldn't give me anything for what we were calling "post-partum depression"). By the time I started and stopped various drugs over the next twelve months, I had gained about twenty pounds and wasn't sleeping that much better. I was on the maximum dosages of Effexor, Wellbutrin, Ambien, and Zoloft. I got the great idea to take myself off my birth control pills since I was taking so much other medication. When the doctor found out about that, he advised me to stop all of my other medication immediately due to the risk of birth defects should I become pregnant. I had read, however, that a person should "step down" off psychotropic drugs so I made my own careful plan to do so over the course of a few weeks.

I remember sensations that I can only describe as electrical currents going down my limbs each time I decreased my dosage. I took my very last dose on a Friday and showed up for Bible study the following Tuesday as usual. Craig dropped off the kids and me since my car was in the shop. Barbara had graciously offered to drive us home. After Bible study ended, I remember someone hugging me good-bye. I did not reciprocate. Instead, I stood with my arms straight by my side while she wrapped her arms around me. I really don't remember much about the ride home with Barbara either.

However, as we pulled into my driveway, I began to panic. In my numbness and fright, I cried out to Barbara, "Don't leave me. Please don't leave me. I am going to kill myself or my children!" Needless to say, she did not leave me but stayed with me until Craig got home. Barbara told me later how, after she left, she went home and prayed for me. Although not her usual practice, she lay prostrate on the floor, begging God to move on my behalf.

I am thankful that Barbara showed her love for me in such a tender, yet powerful, way. God answered her prayers. Prayer is a high privilege and it is a spiritual discipline of which we are to avail ourselves. It is in prayer that we see the way in which God's sovereignty and man's responsibility come together. I believe strongly in the sovereignty of God. I know that what God ordains He will bring to pass (Isa. 46:11). No one can thwart His will (Job 42:2). I also know, however, that although God ordains the end, He has also ordained the means to that end. One of those means is prayer. As Charles H. Spurgeon has so beautifully stated: "Prayer is the slender nerve that moveth the muscles of Omnipotence."[4] God moved on my behalf in a powerful way that day.

We have to be careful about the way that we approach God. Prayer is not coming to God with a "wish list," expecting Him to give us everything that we desire. God is not a celestial Santa Claus who desires to grant us our every wish. Rather, prayer is communion with God; it is talking to our Heavenly Father. It involves praise, confession, supplication, and submission to God's will. We must pray according to His will if we want Him to hear us (1 John 5:14–15). I do not believe in the "name-it-and-claim-it" theology. So, when I say we must pray according to His will, I am talking about His will as revealed in Scripture. I often encourage women to pray the Scriptures, if they want to pray according to God's will.[5]

There is no doubt in my mind that the privilege of prayer is too often neglected. We all forget what an honor it is to go into the very throne room of God. This access to God the Father is only made possible because of the Person and finished work of our Lord Jesus Christ. When Christ gave up His spirit after completing His sacrificial atoning death, the veil of the temple was torn in two from top to bottom (Matt. 27:51). The book of Hebrews makes it clear that now God's children have access directly to Him: "Therefore, brethren, since we have confidence to enter the holy place by the blood of Jesus, by a new and living way which He

---

4   Charles Spurgeon, *The Power In Prayer* (New Kensington, PA: Whitaker House, 1996), 55.
5   We highly recommend Donald Whitney's book *Praying The Bible* (Wheaton, IL: Crossway Publishing Company, 2015).

inaugurated for us through the veil, that is, His flesh, and since we have a great priest over the house of God, let us draw near with a sincere heart in full assurance of faith . . ." (Heb. 10:19–22a).

As children of God, we can approach the throne of Almighty God to "receive mercy and find grace to help in time of need" (Heb. 4:16). The day Barbara lay prostrate in prayer for me was truly a "time of need." Barbara could not change my suicidal desires, but she went to the throne of grace to find mercy for me.

However, the truth of the matter is that every waking moment of our lives is a "time of need" because, apart from Christ, we can do nothing (John 15:5). Indeed, ". . . in Him all things hold together" (Col. 1:17). Prayer is one way we express this dependence upon God. I have heard it said that the absence of prayer is the presence of pride. In other words, prayer shows my dependence upon God. Conversely, the absence of prayer shows my prideful dependence upon myself.

Prayer also exposes our spiritual maturity. Dr. Martyn Lloyd-Jones states it this way:

> Our ultimate position as Christians is tested by the character of our prayer life. It is more important than knowledge and understanding. Do not imagine that I am detracting from the importance of knowledge. I spend most of my life trying to show the importance of having a knowledge of truth and an understanding of it. That is vitally important. There is only one thing that is more important, and that is prayer . . . . If all my knowledge does not lead me to prayer, there is something wrong somewhere.[6]

The truths Barbara had been taught about the attributes of God—namely, His sovereignty, His mercy, and His grace—are the teachings that drove her to pray for me that day.

God, in His mercy, spared me and my children. I was not left alone with my kids nor did I drive for almost three weeks while I detoxed—during my depression, I consistently thought of driving my car off the road. I later found out that I was experiencing severe side effects known as akathisia, which are common when

6   Dr. Martyn Lloyd-Jones as quoted in Dr. Wayne Mack's book *Reaching The Ear of God* (Phillipsburg, NJ: P&R Publishing Company, 2004), 32–33.

a person first starts taking antidepressants or when a person goes through the process of coming off these medications. These side effects include a desperate feeling of restlessness and anxiety. The Collins English Dictionary defines these symptoms as the "inability to sit still because of uncontrollable movement caused by reaction to drugs."[7] This agitation often makes a person feel overwhelmed and suicidal. The Lord graciously spared all of us heartbreak and restored me over the coming months.

It was through this incident that my relationship with Barbara was firmly cemented. When I found out that Barbara had prayed for me prostrate before the Lord, I remember thinking how much she must love me to do that. It is comforting to know that someone intends to pray for you. I don't want to diminish that. However, to know that someone is beseeching the Lord for you, laboring in prayer before Him for you, well, that's pretty powerful.

Knowing Barbara's care and concern for me always informed my perception of how she viewed me and treated me. This knowledge enabled me to always think the best of Barbara, giving her the benefit of the doubt. It also helped me accept Barbara's counsel even when it was hard to hear. Moreover, our communication was unhindered and honest because of this perception. I had no fear of sharing anything with her or asking her anything. Knowing she loved me even gave me the freedom to confess my sins to her (James 5:16). For example, we both remember a day when I was telling her about a particular sin that I was struggling to overcome. I expected her to be shocked. However, with no change in her facial expression, Barbara calmly said, "You have not thought of any new sin." In essence, she was comforting me with instruction from 1 Corinthians 10:13 which states: "No temptation has overtaken you but such as is common to man; and God is faithful, who will not allow you to be tempted beyond what you are able, but with the temptation will provide the way of escape also, so that you will be able to endure it." Knowing her love for me fostered this unhindered communication. Proverbs 27:9b says it best: ". . . a man's counsel is sweet to his friend."

As our relationship was further cemented, we seemed more

---

7   *Collins English Dictionary*–Complete and Unabridged (San Francisco, CA: HarperCollins Publishers, 2003).

united in spirit and intent on one purpose (Phil. 2:2). We both knew that our relationship would prove to spur us on more intentionally in our walk with God. It has been, for the most part, one of pushing each other forward in our pursuit of God.

We believe the quality that makes our relationship unique is this intentional and purposeful seeking of the Lord together. Added to that is the fact that we are focused on ministry together, serving God and serving His people. It has never been about "our" friendship. Our relationship together was not cemented through common interests such as cooking, hiking, or shopping. We were not drawn toward each other because of any particular character trait that we saw in the other person. We certainly were not united because we are the same age. (Oh, how I love to remind Barbara that she is almost twenty years older than I!) We are convinced it is for one sole reason that God providentially gave us this discipleship relationship. That reason is a Person—Jesus Christ. Because both of us are united to Christ, we are, therefore, united together as sisters in Christ. He has always been the focal point of our relationship. By His grace, He will remain that way as we continue our journey.

For Further Thought

1. Are you experiencing the richness of true fellowship, true *koinonia*? If so, spend some time thanking God for that blessing. If not, can you identify a reason for this? How can you begin to change?

2. Is there a woman with whom you are close that, you know, is making foolish choices? If so, how could you come alongside her in order to help her?

3. Is there a woman you know for whom you should labor in prayer?

4. Consider the quotation from Dr. Martyn Lloyd-Jones concerning the connection between prayer and spiritual maturity. In view of his statement, how mature would you consider yourself to be?

5. We have never met any women who consider their prayer life to be adequate. Assuming this is true of you, would you consider studying Dr. Wayne Mack's book entitled *Reaching The Ear of God* (publisher details given in footnote 7, earlier in this chapter) with a close sister in Christ?

6. Is there a woman with whom you are free to be yourself, one with whom you can be honest and open concerning all matters? We are not encouraging venting; actually, we oppose it (Prov. 29:20). The woman you approach needs to be someone who can give you wise, biblical counsel, without allowing you to sin.

7. Is there a relationship you have that might be a detriment to your growth in Christ? If so, we encourage you to think about how God would have you deal with this relationship. One way would be to approach the woman with biblical suggestions to turn the relationship into one that is mutually edifying. Or, you may have to move graciously away from this relationship. We suggest you pray and seek wise counsel as you move forward.

8. Is there a relationship that you can foster with someone with whom you currently minister? If so, what steps can you take to begin cementing the relationship?

3

A Clear View of the Journey

Be imitators of me, just as I also am of Christ.
(1 Corinthians 11:1)

• • • • • • • • • • • • • •

When people talk to Gina and me about the book we're writing, most understand that we are writing a personal story of discipleship, not just about discipleship. Someone asked us if we were going to define discipleship and explain what discipleship looks like. He went on to ask if we were going to make sure people understood that we did not want to make disciples of or for ourselves. Well, the answer to both of those questions is yes!

The One Thing: Discipleship Defined

The time has come to define discipleship. But first let us make one thing clear: we are not encouraging other women to make disciples of or for themselves. Regrettably, that already occurs in the church. Some exclusively follow one particular person such as a teacher, pastor, or televangelist. They put their ultimate trust in that person. For example, many cults have a particular leader to whom members must affirm allegiance, even to the point that individual members are designated as a "follower of so and so." This type of allegiance to another person is not what the discipleship relationship is about. Although Paul wrote, "Be imitators of me . . ." (1 Cor. 11:1a), he added the clarifying comment, ". . . just as I also am of Christ" (1 Cor. 11:1b). Paul did not merely encourage believers to imitate him or to become his disciple. He wanted to disciple others so that they would follow Christ and become more like their Savior. He was striving to make disciples of Jesus Christ, not himself.

Now that we've made the first point clear, let's clarify something else of importance: the definition of discipleship. We've found it helpful to discuss what something is not before explaining what it is. Let's consider what discipleship is not. As stated in previous chapters, discipleship is not merely a friendship. Friendships are usually based on common interests, a common season of life, or common hobbies. Too often Christian women are drawn to other women whom they can hang out with, whether it's someone to go shopping with, go to movies together, or just go to the park for a playdate. They look for other women with whom they enjoy spending time. It is true there is a bond among friends. However, that type of bond does not reach the depth that exists between sisters in Christ who participate in ministry together and who are students in the school of Christ together. This type of union is spiritual, deep, and rich.

As such, a discipleship relationship supersedes a mere friendship. When Paul wrote to the church in Philippi, he mentions qualities found in relationships that would bring him great joy. He writes, "Therefore if there is any encouragement in Christ, if there is any consolation of love, if there is any fellowship of the Spirit, if any affection and compassion, make my joy complete by being of the same mind, maintaining the same love, united in spirit, intent on one purpose" (Phil. 2:1-2). Paul is encouraging these believers to be like-minded, loving, united in spirit, and intentionally focused on one shared purpose. The word *spirit* here is from the Greek word *súmpsuchos* and means "together . . . soul . . . [in other words] joined together in soul."[8] This type of union goes far beyond simply a friendship and also goes far beyond just the horizontal relationship between two women. This type of relationship is focused on Someone outside and above the human relationship. It is a vertical relationship first. Moreover, it is the focus on the vertical relationship that undergirds and holds together the horizontal relationship.

Gina and I are convinced that our horizontal relationship only exists because of each of our individual and vertical relationships with Christ. As you will see in the next chapter, we really don't have that much in common other than our love for Christ. However, it is our love for Christ and His people that has brought us together and kept us together with very little effort. We know that if our focus had been all about "our" relationship, then our relationship would have suffered much turmoil. (We are both very opinionated!) Our relationship is only as strong as we are united in spirit and intent on one

---

8 Zodhiates, *Key Study Bible*, 1877.

purpose outside of ourselves. Of course, that purpose is to glorify God and seek to promote His Kingdom on earth, not our own (Isa. 43:7; Matt. 6:33).

How are we as believers to carry out this purpose? Well, have you ever wondered why God does not just take us to heaven the minute we get saved? If heaven is our real home and God is our heavenly Father, then why doesn't God just instantly bring His children home? If God snatched us home right after conversion, then we would be perfectly holy and not have to go through progressive sanctification.[9] We would instantly be just like our Savior (1 John 3:2). Part of the answer to these questions is found in Matthew 28:19-20. In some of His final instructions to His disciples, Jesus said, "Go therefore and make disciples of all the nations, baptizing them in the name of the Father and the Son and the Holy Spirit, teaching them to observe all that I commanded you; and lo, I am with you always, even to the end of the age."

It is sad to say that these verses are often misunderstood and, therefore, misapplied. They are often used to challenge believers to "go" and evangelize and make converts. However, the main verb in this command is "make disciples." The participles modifying this main verb are "going," "baptizing," and "teaching." In other words, as we are going along our way through life, we are to be making disciples, and then baptizing them, and teaching them. In fact, the word "go" in our English Bibles would be better "translated 'having gone,' suggesting that this requirement is not so much a command as an assumption."[10] As we are going, we are to be making disciples of Jesus Christ.

The words "make disciples" in this text are the translation of the Greek word *mathēteúō*, which comes from a root word that means a learner or a disciple. "*Mathēteúō* means not only to learn, but to become attached to one's teacher and to become his follower in doctrine and conduct of life."[11] A disciple, therefore,

---

9   There are three aspects of sanctification—past, present, and future (1 Cor. 6:11; 2 Cor. 3:18; Heb. 12:23). We are referring to the present ongoing process of sanctification which is the "progressive work of God and man that makes us more and more free from sin and like Christ in our actual lives." See Wayne Grudem, *Systematic Theology* (Grand Rapids, MI: Zondervan, 1994), 746.

10   John MacArthur, *The MacArthur New Testament Commentary: Matthew 24–28* (Chicago, IL: Moody Publishers, 1989), 342.

11   Zodhiates, *Key Study Bible*, 1853.

is someone who wants to learn about Jesus Christ, who He is and what He requires. She attaches herself to the risen Christ, studies His Word, and tries to learn how to walk in His steps. A disciple does not merely come to Jesus for salvation, but she keeps coming to Him to grow and become more like Him. She attaches herself to her ultimate Teacher. She desires to be taught all of Jesus' commandments.

Moreover, a true disciple wants to learn to observe all of Jesus' commandments. The word *"observe"* in Matthew 28:20 is *tēréō* and comes from a word that means a warden or a guard. It means to "keep an eye on, watch, and hence to guard, keep, obey."[12] Thus, a true disciple of Jesus Christ desires more than just head knowledge of His commands. She is eager to obey those commands. A true disciple of Jesus Christ has the same heart attitude as the Psalmist when he wrote: "I considered my ways And turned my feet to Your testimonies. I hastened and did not delay To keep Your commandments" (Ps. 119:59–60). This is the attitude that a true disciple has toward God's commandments.

One of the commands that a true disciple desires to obey is "make disciples." This is a command and not an option. Jesus is not just making a suggestion. Jesus never commanded us to go and make "friends." A follower of Jesus desires to make other disciples of Jesus Christ and teach them all that she has learned about her Savior. This discipleship is best accomplished through what Jay Adams calls the "with him" method.

Teaching through discipleship is not merely academic. Jay Adams writes, "When Jesus chose His disciples, it does *not* say that He chose them to attend His lectures . . . but, rather, 'to be with Him' (Mark 3:14)"[13] This implies that a discipleship relationship involves time spent together, time "doing life together." So, the discipler will instruct but also spend time with the person she is discipling. For example, Gina not only came to the Bible study that I was teaching, but we also spent time together outside the classroom. We painted rooms in her house; she helped me with

---

12   Spiros Zodhiates, *The Complete Word Study Dictionary: New Testament* (Electronic Edition, Chattanooga, TN: AMG Publishers, 2000).

13   Jay E. Adams, *A Theology Of Christian Counseling: More Than Redemption* (Grand Rapids, MI: Zondervan, 1979), 88.

my daughter's wedding; I watched her young children when she had other appointments, etc. Our discipleship relationship did not just involve "lectures" in Bible study, but we spent informal time just doing life together.

When I first met Gina and got to know her, I realized that she was a young believer who needed discipleship. This recognition led me to want to teach Gina what other faithful believers had taught me. I have a card on my desk that says, "How can I help _____ become more like Jesus?" This is the goal of discipleship, and this is what I wanted for Gina. I wanted to teach Gina how to observe all that God has said. I wanted the two of us to grow together in our knowledge of God, what He has done and what He has promised to do. I wanted to teach her what God requires of a woman, a mother, a keeper of her home, and even a church member. I wanted her to learn how to resolve conflicts biblically and how to respond to trials in a manner that would honor God. So, we studied a biblical theology of suffering together, a theology that God would eventually ask Gina to live out as she encountered the trial of bone marrow cancer. Ultimately, I wanted Gina to learn to please her Savior and become more like Him (2 Cor. 3:18).

From her side, Gina wanted to learn. She wanted to know what was required of her. As a learner (disciple), she wanted to know how to be pleasing to God in the various roles He had given her. Gina was teachable in that she did not argue with the Scriptures but rather submitted to the authority of God's Word. She desired to obey even when it was difficult for her. Let me explain, using two rather lengthy examples. These examples will illustrate not only Gina's willingness to obey God but also the importance of the "with him" method of discipleship.

Having learned how to be reconciled biblically with other believers through my studies at The Master's University, I then, in turn, wanted to teach Gina. I taught Gina the difference between saying "I'm sorry" and asking for forgiveness after sinning against someone. Apologizing is the world's substitute for biblical confession. "An apology is an inadequate, humanistic substitute for the real thing. Nowhere do the Scriptures require, or even encourage, apologizing. To say 'I'm sorry' is a human dodge for doing what God has commanded."[14] Saying "I am sorry" is just dumping your feelings on someone else.

If merely saying "I am sorry" is inadequate, then what should we do? The real question is what would God have us to do when we have sinned against someone? The biblical requirement is confession and then asking for forgiveness.[15] When we have sinned against someone, we should ask them this simple question: "Will you forgive me?" "When a person asks, 'Will you forgive me?' he has punted; the ball has changed hands, and a response is now required of the one addressed. The onus of responsibility has shifted from the one who did the wrong to the one who has been wronged. Both parties, therefore, are required to put the matter in the past."[16] The only correct godly response is "Yes, I forgive you."

When a person says, "I forgive you," she is making a promise to forgive as God in Christ has forgiven her (Eph. 4:32; Isa. 43:25; Mic. 7:18–19; Jer. 31:34). This covenant of forgiveness includes four promises:

- I will not dwell on this incident.
- I will not bring up this incident again and use it against you.
- I will not talk to others about this incident.
- I will not let this incident stand between us or hinder our personal relationship.[17]

I wanted Gina to put these truths into practice after she and Craig had sinned against each other with their words. Gina was afraid to do this, afraid of Craig's response, afraid that the conversation would escalate the conflict. She was so upset at the prospect of doing this that she was crying on the phone as she spoke to me, repeatedly telling me that she couldn't resolve their conflict by applying these truths. I patiently continued to exhort Gina to obey. I told Gina that I believed she really did want to obey the Lord. I role played with her, instructing her and helping

---

14   Ibid., 221.

15   To learn how to give a thorough, biblical confession, we highly recommend following the 7 A's of Confession as taught in Ken Sande's book *The Peacemaker* (Grand Rapids, MI: Baker Book House, 2004). In particular, see pages 126–134 found in Chapter 6.

16   Adams, *A Theology Of Christian Counseling*, 222.

17   Sande, *The Peacemaker*, 209.

her choose a good time to talk with Craig. Despite her fear, Gina approached Craig. They were able both to extend and receive biblical forgiveness for their unkind words. In doing so, they experienced true biblical reconciliation.

In telling me about the conversation with Craig, Gina marveled at how unemotional it had been and how easy it was. Moreover, since true biblical reconciliation makes the relationship better than it was before, Craig and Gina experienced this in their relationship perhaps for the first time. Reconciling in this biblical manner rather than the world's inadequate substitute became a habit for them that allowed their relationship to grow spiritually. Craig and Gina taught their children these principles as well.

As mentioned previously, I also wanted to teach Gina how to respond to trials in a manner that would honor God. As she grew in her theology of suffering, she would have the opportunity to practice the truths that she learned and I had the opportunity to minister to her in tangible ways, not merely instruct her. Moreover, I had the joy of watching my "daughter" in the faith excel in honoring God in a trial.

The apostle John wrote, "I have no greater joy than this, to hear of my children walking in the truth" (3 John 1:4). I had such joy as I watched Gina apply all that we had learned about suffering and trials when she was diagnosed with a rare bone marrow cancer (Waldenstrom Macroglobulinemia). Her husband had lost his job a month previously when she started showing symptoms of a medical problem. She was growing tired very easily, losing her breath when walking, and her skin tone was yellowish. After much urging, Gina finally went to her primary care doctor to get some blood work done. The blood work showed that she needed to get to an oncologist immediately for further testing, including a bone marrow biopsy. On the day that Gina received the results of her tests, I was in the room along with her husband and our friend, Erin. Her oncologist looked at her and said, "Your biopsy shows that you have bone marrow cancer." Gina did not hesitate to answer him by saying, "I am so sorry that you are having to tell me this." The doctor was stunned and looked over at the three of us. He then reiterated, "No, you are the one we are concerned about." Gina quickly replied, "I know but this has to be hard on you to have to tell me this."

I think I can safely say that I would imagine that he has never heard such a gracious reply from a patient who has just been told that she has cancer. Holding back tears, I watched Gina respond to her trial in such a manner that was not full of self-pity, fear, or hopelessness. Although not happy about having cancer, she did count it all joy as she encountered this trial (James 1:2). She had become so God-centered and others-centered that she was truly concerned for the hardship that the oncologist was experiencing as he had to be the bearer of difficult news. As I reflected back on when we first met, I realized what a trophy of God's grace Gina had become. God had changed her from a selfish, self-focused individual to a God-fearing woman. What a joy it was to see how God's grace had changed her.

Gina received several blood transfusions and chemotherapy, which has sent her bone marrow cancer into remission. The thing about this type of cancer, however, is that it cannot be cured. Eventually, it will come back. (And it did. Gina discusses her first relapse with cancer in chapter 4.) During the two years that Gina went through her treatment for cancer, I watched her glorify God in her submission to the trial that He had providentially sent into her life. She continued to be focused on God and His Kingdom, not on herself. She actually kept serving in our church as she was physically able, serving God and serving others. She continued to be others-centered, not self-centered. Our friend, Ann, who took Gina to most of her chemo treatments, mentioned how Gina would minister to others even in the chemo room. She would encourage the other patients. She would ask them about themselves and how she could pray for them. Gina obeyed God's commands by refusing to complain and rather resolving to give thanks. She took God seriously when He said, "Rejoice always; pray without ceasing; in everything give thanks; for this is God's will for you in Christ Jesus" (1 Thess. 5:16–18).

By being quick to submit to God's commands, Gina demonstrated what a true disciple's attitude should be to the authority of God's Word. As Isaiah says, our attitude to the Word should be one of fear and trembling (Isa. 66:2). As a godly Puritan once said, "Now let the word of the Lord come; and if I had six hundred necks, I would bow them all to the authority of it."[18]

When one has found a woman who has a high view of the Scriptures—in particular, the authority of the Scriptures—then one can disciple her. This is what a discipleship relationship throughout our journeys is all about!

18   Matthew Henry, *The Quest for Meekness and Quietness of Spirit* (Morgan, PA: Soli Deo Gloria Publications, 1996), 19.

For Further Thought

1. Are you a learner (disciple) of Jesus Christ? If so, how can you continue to cultivate this relationship? List five ways you can grow in this area.

2. If you are unsure of your relationship with Jesus Christ, please see Appendix A: Martha Peace's Salvation Worksheets.

3. As you follow Christ, are you making disciples as you go? If not, how can you begin to obey this command of our Lord?

4. Can you identify a woman whom you know or with whom you have acquaintance whom you could follow as she follows Christ? List her Christlike traits.

5. Can you identify a woman who shares your passion for the things of God? How can you help her to become a better learner (disciple) of Christ?

6. After reading about biblical forgiveness, is there someone with whom you need to seek true reconciliation? Schedule a good time to do this soon.

7. If you, or a friend, receive a cancer diagnosis, we would highly recommend a booklet by John Piper entitled *Don't Waste Your Cancer* (Wheaton, IL: Crossway, 2011).

8. Examine your attitude toward the Word of God based on Isaiah 66:2. How are you doing? List at least two specific ways in which you can cultivate a proper awe for God's Word.

4

The Body Is Necessary for the Journey

*"We urge you, brethren, admonish the unruly, encourage the
fainthearted, help the weak, be patient with everyone."*
(1 Thessalonians 5:14)

• • • • • • • • • • • • • • •

I, Gina, went to my oncologist a month early because I was
afraid. Crushing headaches had become my constant companion. I was often short of breath again. I went alone, thinking maybe my blood counts were down just a little. Boy, was I wrong. This
time, though, I was mad. The blood tests showed once again that
the cancer had come back; another bone marrow biopsy would
be needed to show if it was the same type or not. I was immediately scheduled for a blood transfusion the next day. It was not
how I had planned to spend the day before Thanksgiving. It was
not what I planned period. I had pumpkin pie to make, Christmas
presents to buy, decorations to put up. Didn't the Lord know how
busy I was? What about my counselees? Who would minister to
them now? I also had a new job waiting for me. I was supposed
to start the Monday after Thanksgiving. Didn't God know this job
would provide my family with a little bit of extra income but,
more importantly, group insurance? Didn't He care?

The Journey Intensifies

I suppose no one is ever really prepared for a cancer diagnosis.
I know I wasn't back in 2012. Maybe due to ignorance or a lack
of oxygen to my brain due to low blood volume but probably because of God's grace, I did not strive against what the Lord had
providentially brought into our lives the first time around. This
time was different though. I knew what was coming my way: all
the doctors' appointments, the neuropathy from the treatments,
the various side effects and fatigue. All the needles! If I'm honest,
those things were not what upset me the most (although the needles were a close second). I was mad because cancer was going
to interrupt the agenda I had set for myself, namely, starting my
new job. I was too sick to work. I viewed this round of cancer as

an interruption to my plans and goals. I had forgotten what Jesus said is needed in order to be His disciple: ". . . If anyone wishes to come after Me, he must deny himself, and take up his cross daily and follow Me" (Luke 9:23).

This is going to sound crazy but what was worse this time around was that I now knew that my disease was treatable. My body responded well to my prior treatment so I assumed that this round of treatment would put me into a remission as well. As I saw it, cancer would continue to come into my life when I didn't expect it, and I would have to undergo treatments each time. The interruptions would continue and I would be subject to them again and again. I presumed on the Lord; it didn't occur to me that He didn't have to heal me. I had forgotten that the "mind of man plans his way, But the LORD directs his steps" (Prov. 16:9).

At my first transfusion appointment, I panicked and lashed out at the two nurses who had come to take care of me. I had taken off my wrist band identifying my blood type. This oversight meant an extra needle stick and wasted time. I begged them to let Craig go home to get it from the trashcan where I had thrown it. After calming me down, they explained that they could get the information from the lab and that they would try their best to limit my sticks to just one.

After the transfusion was underway (it took two tries to find a good vein), I was able to reflect on how I had treated those ladies whose sole purpose was to help me. I began to cry when I considered what a poor testimony I had been for the Lord. I resolved then with God's grace to respond differently in the future. I was able to speak with each of them that day, telling them I was sorry for my response. For future help, I asked a group of friends from church to pray for me every time I knew I was going to have an IV. They would text me Bible verses, reminding me of God's presence, kindness, and love toward me. Barbara encouraged me to recite a verse to myself and remind myself that the pain I was experiencing was nothing compared to what Christ experienced on the cross. All these seemingly small things were a big comfort to me. Sometimes I winced or cried out in pain due to the needles, but I was never again unkind to anyone who was caring for me. I am thankful to the Lord for that.

These same ladies helped me in other ways as well during my treatments. Two of them came over to my house regularly to help me clean. One of them commented that when we were together, it always wound up as a counseling session. I laughed, stating, "That's just life." Two others from my small group helped me with my cooking responsibilities at church. I didn't have the stamina or strength to do the job on my own so they would arrange for someone to care for their kids and then come in a few hours early to prepare salad, make drinks, or set up the buffet line. I have another friend who sent me both cards and ecards throughout the week. I've kept every one.

God saw fit to put my cancer into a second remission. My oncologist suggested a meeting with a transplant specialist since this remission would more than likely be shorter than the first one, which lasted four years. Craig, Barbara, and I met with a doctor specializing in my disease for over two hours. We found out much about the transplant procedure itself and also what it would require beforehand as well as after. We immediately asked our church family to pray with us concerning such a big decision. I had to undergo tests covering my whole system to make sure my body could handle the stress of a transplant. Barbara and our friend, Ann, accompanied me to appointments when Craig could not be with me. I also had to self-administer shots in order to stimulate my stem cells for the collection. I asked a friend who is a registered nurse to do that for me; however, she actually took the time to teach me how to do it. While it was not easy, I was eventually able to give myself those shots!

Some appointments lasted the whole day. For example, I was scheduled at the hospital to have a special catheter put in my chest and then go upstairs for the stem cell collection early in the morning the day after Mother's Day. Barbara and I had planned to stay at a hotel the night of Mother's Day so as not to be late to the appointment. This plan would still have given us time to spend with our families on Mother's Day. However, the Friday evening before, I received a call stating that I had to go down for blood work at 12 o'clock the day before the procedure. Needless to say, Barbara went down with me, missing her Mother's Day celebration.

In order to have the transplant, I needed someone with me at all times, not only in the hospital but also for two weeks after it, staying at a hotel close to the hospital. Barbara organized it all. She took the first week; Ann took the next. My daughter filled in when Ann had to work. Barbara also got another friend to stay with me when all three of them had other commitments. In choosing this other person, Barbara's concern was that this person would be able to minister to me spiritually as well as physically. A few friends from church also came to bring me food during my hospital stay.

Thankfully, I didn't have to stay the two weeks near the hospital as planned. I was doing so well that the transplant team allowed me to go home. However, I required twenty-four-hour supervision in case a problem arose very suddenly. I could not go to my own home since all three of my family members worked and couldn't provide the attention I needed. Barbara and Jack graciously opened their home to me. As I'm typing, I've been with them almost five weeks. Lord willing, I will go home next week. It is not an exaggeration to say that, without Barbara, I would not have been able to have the transplant.

Why am I discussing in such depth my second session with cancer? First, I want to illustrate in vivid detail what we have been saying about the "with-Him" method. Discipleship is more than instructing others verbally. Discipleship is *verbal instruction* but it is also *visible instruction* as you walk beside one another through life. Paul encouraged believers when he said, "The things you have learned and received and heard and *seen in me*, practice these things, and the God of peace will be with you" (Phil. 4:9, emphasis added). These believers had been instructed by Paul, but he had also modeled the truths that he wanted them to learn. This modeling only happens as we spend time together. The details of the story also emphasize the importance of the body of Christ in the life of a believer who is struggling, either spiritually or physically.

During the conversations Barbara and I had between all my early appointments when I was diagnosed the second time, she recognized that I was growing bitter toward the Lord. I was really struggling to trust the Lord concerning the job that I had been offered and had had to turn down due to my cancer. My family needed the additional income. Barbara would comment that, at that time, it was best for me not to have that job otherwise God would have given it to me, that cancer was His plan for me at that time, and that He would continue to provide for my family. I would respond with something to this effect, "yeah, but. . . ." Basically, I started arguing with her while, at the same time, denying that my desire for a job had become inordinate. She gently but firmly reproved me, exhorting me to repent of my unbiblical thinking. When I would say "I just don't see how this is good" or "how God will provide," she would show me how I was leaning on my own understanding. She reminded me of a familiar verse from Proverbs: "Trust in the LORD with all your heart And do not lean on your own understanding" (Prov. 3:5). She told me that my understanding was like leaning on a *papier-mâché* wall which could not hold me up. She was right; the *papier-mâché* wall was collapsing!

I persisted in this sin for a while. Thankfully, by God's grace, I repented. My family's financial situation has gotten worse. But I am continually amazed at the Lord's kindness toward us as shown by our brothers' and sisters' generosity. After hearing about our situation, people in our church body, some anonymously and some personally, have given Craig and me monetary gifts to help with the expenses associated with a transplant. When I consider all the ways in which my family and I have been helped by our church family over these last eight months, it is astounding and very humbling. They "one-anothered" us well![19] Interestingly, many of the people who ministered so faithfully to us during my trial were people whom we had previously ministered to or with whom we had ministered.

I am increasingly convinced that the church, the body of Christ, is absolutely necessary for our spiritual well-being. In fact, it is critical. Many of us would give assent to this truth. But do we put ourselves into a local church where we can actively live it out, both in giving and in receiving? Consider Christian in John Bunyan's book *The Pilgrim's Progress*. He is an example of one who grows in his understanding of the importance of the church in the

---

19 For more on how "one-anothering" can help the discipleship relationship, see Chapter 7.

life of a believer as he matures in his faith. In Chapter 5, Christian sees the Delectable Mountains, which represent the church, from a distance. Yet in Chapter 12, he is at the Mountains, eating and drinking freely of all that is available. What's the difference? Dr. Wayne Mack explains this difference in his book, *Christian Life Issues* Volume 2: *The Christian Journey Continued and Concluded*, which is a commentary on John Bunyan's *The Pilgrim's Progress*. Mack states that Bunyan is communicating this truth:

> [T]he older we get in the Christian life, if we're truly Christians, the more we should grow in appreciation for the ministry of the church. In other words, he is saying that Christian has come to a new and fuller appreciation for the church. The further he goes along in his Christian life, the more he is aware of the importance and value of the church, and the more he understands the role it should play in his life . . . Our experience of the church, the body of Christ, just gets better and better and more and more valuable and precious to us the longer we are Christians. As younger Christians, many times we know intellectually about the importance of the church for our lives. But, it is one thing to know something cognitively about the church, and it's different to begin to understand how much we need the people of God, how much we need preaching, and how much we need the encouragement of fellowship.[20]

My journey includes cancer; maybe yours does too. No matter what, though, I pray you have seen that the body is essential to the journey. One will be crippled if one tries to make the journey alone.[21]

---

20   Dr. Wayne A. Mack, *Christian Life Issues* Vol. 2: *The Christian Journey Continued and Concluded* (Bemidji, MN: Focus Publishing, 2017), 223.

21   My cancer did return for a third time in September 2018; it is currently in remission once again through the treatment of a daily "chemo" pill.

For Further Thought

....

1. Describe a time when your plans and agenda were providentially hindered or changed by the Lord.

2. How did you respond?

3. How would God have you respond according to Luke 9:23–24?

4. In this chapter, Gina tells specifically of how the body of Christ ministered to her. Are you actively ministering to others in your local church? Make a list of those people.

5. Are you allowing others into your life to intimately minister to you? If not, would you consider that you should humble yourself and let others serve you in very specific ways?

6. Can you see the difference between mere *verbal instruction* and *visible instruction* using the "with-Him" method? List three reasons why the *visible instruction* is necessary.

7. Gina gave the example of Barbara having to reprove her for unbiblical thinking. Do you have an intimate sister who will reprove and admonish you when necessary? If not, is there someone to whom you can give the freedom to reprove you when necessary?

8. Are you endangering yourself of stunting your growth in Christ by not being actively and intimately involved in your local church? If so, list three ways in which you are going to rectify this dangerous position in which you find yourself.

5

Looking for Other Disciples to Join the Journey

And He gave some as apostles, and some as prophets, and some as evangelists, and some as pastors and teachers, for the equipping of the saints for the work of service, to the building up of the body of Christ.
(Ephesians 4:11–12)

• • • • • • • • • • • • • •

Most of you probably have a recipe for spaghetti sauce. I am guessing that your recipe would be similar to mine. Even with slight variations, we would still call it "sauce" because we would all recognize it as sauce. One would think that one could expect this uniformity in recipes for lasagna. Not if your name is Barbara Enter, however. I do have a recipe for lasagna. In spite of that name, my recipe is not remotely close to what some would agree is actually lasagna. My "lasagna" doesn't include ricotta or even the Southern standby, cottage cheese. While Gina concedes that my (non-Italian) family loves my "lasagna," it is NOT what Gina calls lasagna.

Gina has repeatedly told me to call my recipe anything I want but, "just don't call it lasagna!" Literally, this has been a running joke between us for years. It was settled by a friend who suggested we rename my dish "Barb-sagna." Brilliant!

Diversity in Unity

Why the story? After all, you'd think that something as common as lasagna would not highlight differences between two people. But it does. We have hinted at our differences in preceding chapters. However, I want to highlight our differences to show that a discipleship relationship is not based on certain commonalities but on being joined together in Christ. The concept of commonality or compatibility as the basis for Christian relationships is so culturally ingrained. But I want to dispel the misconception that this is the foundation for a discipleship relationship. Even if you are extremely different from one another, you can experience a close relationship with those you disciple and those who disciple you, if you are careful to whom you attach yourself.

Gina and I have explained that, when our relationship began, the obvious differences between us were age and spiritual maturity. Those weren't the only differences. Our backgrounds were radically different, and when our relationship began we were in different stages of life as well. My children were in high school and college; Gina's were just being born. Because of socio-economic differences between our families, we did not travel on vacation together, buy gifts for each other, or go shopping together very often, all activities that "close friends" do. I enjoy antiquing; Gina hates it. I don't go to the mailbox without make-up on just like a true Southern girl. Gina only recently began wearing make-up in earnest after having to get her hair cut short before chemo. I am not a foodie. For Gina, it's all about the food. Every family gathering or holiday has traditional foods that must be served (She did marry a chef after all!).

Please get my point: while these things are interesting, they are not essential to the type of relationship I am talking about. The only commonality in a discipleship relationship that truly matters is Jesus Christ, specifically that both women desire to live their lives in a manner that proclaims the excellencies of Him who called them out of darkness into His marvelous light (1 Peter 2:9). The key that must also be remembered is that the commonality between two sisters in Christ is based on the two of you being "one souled."

When Paul writes to the Philippian church, he encourages them to conduct themselves in a "manner worthy of the gospel of Christ" (Phil. 1:27a). He goes on to say that part of this worthy conduct is "standing firm in one spirit, with one mind striving together for the faith of the gospel" (Phil. 1:27b). The word *mind* in this text comes from the Greek word *psuché*, which is often translated "soul." The soul is the immaterial part of us which is the seat of our desires, thoughts, and emotions. Paul is encouraging these believers to be like-minded in their attitudes concerning life and godliness. This is the type of person with whom you want to pursue God.

I would caution you not to limit yourself by thinking that your disciple or the one who disciples you has to fit a certain profile.

In fact, it took Gina quite a few years to figure this out. For a long time, she was looking for her own "Gina" to disciple because she so appreciated an older woman discipling her and encouraging her growth in the Lord. She wanted to pour herself into other women as had been done to her.

She began praying that the Lord would send her a "Gina." I reminded her that this kind of discipleship relationship could not be forced. Our relationship had been knit together by the Lord. She persisted in her prayers and continued to look for her "Gina." However, she put too many restrictions on her "Gina," trying to replicate our relationship. For instance, she thought she had to be younger in age and need lots of biblical instruction. There were a few times when she would call me and say, "I think I found my Gina" after taking various women to lunch. She would soon be disappointed, however, as she tried to cram each one into a certain mold for discipleship.

Once, someone offered to be her "Gina." She responded by telling this lady that she couldn't be her "Gina" because she was not young enough to take care of her in her old age. I had to gently rebuke her for her insensitive statement and then all three of us had a hearty laugh. Thankfully, this same woman has become one of Gina's dearest friends and even helped to take care of her when she was diagnosed with cancer.

Gina finally realized that she did have a few other women whom she was discipling. Some were older than she was; some were younger. Some were widowed; others were in great marriages; and some were even divorced. She realized that she had missed the richness of these relationships because she was wrongly looking to reproduce our relationship.

Because she had her own standard for a discipleship relationship—a sort of "one size fits all"—she almost missed all of the "Ginas" whom God had given her. She finally realized that she would never have the exact type of discipleship relationship that we shared, and that that was just fine. This fact does not subtract from or negate the uniqueness of her other discipleship relationships. In fact, it makes each relationship better because she is not imposing an expectation on the other person that the person cannot possibly meet. Gina is not trying to put someone into a mold. Instead, she is enjoying the uniqueness of each relationship.

As a result of these insights, she has quit looking for her ideal "Gina." Instead, she is enjoying her relationships with Ann, Lynda, Erin, Sally, Crystal, Jennifer, and others. As we all aim to rightly relate to one another in the Lord, there is no jealousy. What's left is just a thankfulness that the Lord has given us to one another to help us in our sanctification.

However, I want to add a word of caution here. While you don't want to limit the discipleship relationship based on a certain profile, you do want to make sure you are not attaching yourself to the wrong person. If that last statement seems contradictory, hear me out first. While there is no perfect Christian, you want to seek out someone who is endeavoring to make it her goal to be pleasing to the Lord (2 Cor. 5:9). She should not be someone who is "practicing" sin; rather, she should be someone who is striving to put off her sin (1 John 3:7–8).

She should be a woman who is God-centered and not self-centered (Phil. 2:3). If the person you are attaching yourself to is self-centered then you will surely know it. There will be many ways that her selfishness will manifest itself. One, she will have what some people call "big toes." In other words, she will readily and easily get her feelings hurt. Most hurt feelings are a result of being sinfully focused on one's self.[22] For example, if you ask your friend to call you later in the day and she forgets, yet your feelings are "hurt," then you are probably being sinfully self-focused. Perhaps she had a family emergency. Perhaps she had to take care of another responsibility. Or even, perhaps, she simply forgot. Not calling someone back due to these types of reasons should not hurt someone's feelings. If they do, then that person has "big toes."

Another way selfishness manifests itself is through constant, trivial conflicts. It's as though you have to walk around on eggshells when you are around her. You never know if she's going to get mad or not. For instance, if you're at a women's social event where you spend more time talking with someone else than you

---

22   See Martha Peace's book *Damsels In Distress: Biblical Solutions for Problems Women Face* (Phillipsburg, NJ: P&R Publishing Company, 2006), particularly chapter 5: "What Difference Does It Make *What* He Intended? *Hurt Feelings.*"

do with her, she will get mad at you since it's all about her. Or, if you have to cancel an engagement with her for valid reasons, she will get mad at you since it's all about her. Her worldview is such that she wonders why you don't love her as much as she loves herself.[23] Matter of fact, she wonders why no one loves her as much as she loves herself. This love of self will lead to these kinds of silly conflicts.

You certainly do not want to attach yourself to a gossip. The Greek word for gossip is *diabolos*. "We get our English word *devil* from *diabolos*. It means to accuse or to give false information."[24] When a person gossips, she is demonstrating characteristics of Satan. In Revelation 12:10, Satan is called the accuser of the brethren. You would not want to attach yourself to such a person. The book of Proverbs gives us multiple warnings about associating with such a person (Prov. 20:19). Gossip will quickly destroy a relationship. She "who repeats a matter separates intimate friends" (Prov. 17:9b).

Additionally, you would not want to attach yourself to someone who would give you worldly wisdom. Instead, you should seek out someone who would be able to give you biblical wisdom. James gives us clear instruction to help us discern between "worldly" wisdom and wisdom "from above."

> Who among you is wise and understanding? Let him show by his good behavior his deeds in the gentleness of wisdom. But if you have bitter jealousy and selfish ambition in your heart, do not be arrogant and so lie against the truth. This wisdom is not that which comes down from above, but is earthly, natural, demonic. For where jealousy and selfish ambition exist, there is disorder and every evil thing. But the wisdom from above is first pure, then peaceable, gentle, reasonable, full of mercy and good fruits, unwavering, without hypocrisy (James 3:13–17).

Someone who gives worldly wisdom will not help you become more like your Savior. In fact, in the process of giving you worldly

---

23   This statement by Nicolas Ellen was given in a lecture entitled "If Lovin' You Is Right, I Don't Want To be Wrong" at a NANC (ACBC) conference in October, 2010.
24   Peace, *Damsels In Distress*, 30.

wisdom (counsel), she will indeed impede your spiritual growth. For example, her counsel to you would often help you to minimize or justify your sin. Let's say you are struggling with sinful anger toward your children. Worldly wisdom would help you minimize your sin by saying, "Well, you are only human." It would also say, "Don't be so hard on yourself." Additionally, worldly wisdom would help you shift the blame by saying, "Well, it's not your fault because they were being disobedient." Or it would say, "It is all right because it is that time of the month."

Godly wisdom, or counsel, on the other hand, would not help you minimize or justify your sinful response. No, godly wisdom would call you to repentance and remind you that you are 100 percent responsible for your sinful anger because your anger is coming from your own sinful heart (Mark 7:20-23; Matt. 15:18-19). Godly wisdom would remind you that your disobedient children are merely the context that drew out what was already in your heart (Deut. 8:1-3). No one can cause us to sin. We can never say, "You made me mad."

Godly wisdom realizes that we should not minimize, shift blame, or justify our sin. Godly wisdom applies the gospel every day to every sin; therefore, this wisdom calls you back to the cross. It is at the cross that you confess your sin and repent of it. God says that "if we confess our sins, He is faithful and righteous to forgive us our sins and to cleanse us from all unrighteousness" (1 John 1:9). It is when we do this that we again rejoice in the extent of the atonement, which covers all of our sins. As Jerry Bridges reminds us, we should learn to "preach the gospel to ourselves every day."[25]

Let me reiterate. The essential element to keep in mind when you're looking for someone to join you on your journey toward Christlikeness is that the commonality is based on the two of you being "one souled." So, as you're praying about this person for yourself, just focus on pursuing the Lord. One man has said it this way: "Run hard after Christ and then look beside you to see who is running with you." Then move toward that person in meaningful ways as you travel along on your journey.

---

25   Jerry Bridges, *Disciplines of Grace* (Colorado Springs, CO: NavPress, 2006), 26.

For Further Thought

1. Do you have a good recipe for lasagna?

2. The first thing to do when considering any discipleship relationship is to examine yourself. Is the purpose of your life in keeping with the statements in 1 Peter 2:9? Is it your goal to proclaim the excellencies of Jesus Christ?

3. How are you limiting yourself in pursuing a discipleship relationship by thinking the person has to fit a certain profile?

4. Are you imposing an unrealistic expectation on a discipleship relationship? If so, how?

5. When you consider our word of caution, are there warnings you should heed in a relationship you currently have with another person?

6. As you read James 3:13–17, first check yourself. Are you giving wise counsel to others—counsel that is "from above"? Or, are you giving others "worldly" counsel?

7. Examining James 3:13–17 again, consider the counsel that you are receiving. Is it wisdom "from above" or "worldly" wisdom?

8. Are you "running hard after" Jesus? If so, how? If not, what can you start doing to pursue a closer walk with your Savior?

9. When you look beside/around you, who appears to be "running hard after" Jesus?

6

Growing Together in Christ during the Journey

As a result, we are no longer to be children . . . but speaking the
truth in love, we are to grow up in all aspects into Him who is the
head, even Christ.
(Ephesians 4:14–15)

• • • • • • • • • • • • • •

A few years ago, I, Gina, took up vegetable gardening. I attempted to grow what I had been told are foolproof vegetables. I have yet to figure out why my cucumber plants die one year but, on another year, I'll have a bumper crop. The same has happened to my zucchini, but in the reverse. It's truly hit and miss with my garden. I know many people who have gardening down to a science. They can tell you about soil pH and good and bad bugs. These green thumbs cultivate their plants, painstakingly attending to what is seemingly a minute detail. I would bet they usually get good results too.

Growth Takes Place in Community

In First Corinthians, Paul uses imagery from agriculture when he tells us about sharing the gospel with others: he planted the seed, Apollos watered it, but God caused the rebirth, or growth (1 Cor. 3:6). What about after conversion? Do we have to hit and miss as I do in my garden when it comes to growing in Christlikeness? Absolutely not! God, in His kindness, has given us all things necessary for life and godliness (2 Peter 1:3). We don't have to guess when it comes to progressing spiritually.

As Barbara and I grew in Christ together, our relationship developed as well. How did we grow together? There were, and still are, specific things we did to foster this relationship.

One of the foundational ways we grew together was through Barbara verbally instructing me. In the book of Romans, Paul writes that believers are able to admonish one another. "And concerning you, my brethren, I myself also am convinced that you yourselves are full of goodness, filled with all knowledge and able also to admonish one another" (Rom. 15:14). This word *admonish* doesn't usually elicit a positive response. Admonishment is not a negative concept. It comes from the Greek word *nouthetéō* and simply means to "put into the mind."[26] Sometimes it is translated *teach* or *instruct*. In one version, we read that we are able to advise one another. This teaching happened directly in Bible studies but also one on one, as I would call Barbara privately with my questions about doctrine or just the Christian walk in general.

While Barbara did answer many of my questions, in Bible class I had to learn to limit my questions. In other words, I needed to realize that if I dominated the question/answer time, then others would not be able to participate and grow through asking their questions. Privately, however, there was no limit on my questions. Barbara wanted me to have the freedom to ask any question. Barbara has told me that my eagerness to learn was one trait that she appreciated about me. She helped me realize that no question was a "bad" question. However, all of my questions did not have specific answers. While God does provide all of the wisdom we need for life and godliness in general, there will remain specific answers that a believer cannot or will not know. As Deuteronomy 29:29 says, "The secret things belong to the Lord our God, but the things revealed belong to us and to our sons forever, that we may observe all the words of this law."

Additionally, Barbara let me "think out loud." This was a big help. In letting me verbalize my thoughts, I formulated a deeper understanding of biblical concepts as I thought through them and wrestled with them, learning to put the truths into my own words.

Another way Barbara and I grew together is by speaking freely with one another without fear of judgment. While it sounds simple enough, it actually takes patience and skill on both sides. To truly help one another put off sin, we must commit to not being surprised or appalled by sin. I remember Barbara telling me that there was no sin I had done or could do that would make her stop loving me or even think less of me. She often told me that I had not thought of a new sin (1 Cor. 10:13).

So, how can one person have this freedom with another? Since there is now no condemnation for those who are in Christ (Rom. 8:1), why would we think we can treat one another in a

---

26   Zodhiates, *Key Study Bible*, 1859.

condescending way? We can't. Barbara and I are convinced that two people can have this freedom only if they both know the depravity of their own hearts and the deceitfulness of sin. This belief also includes the realization that, apart from the grace of God, one is fully capable of the same sin. At the same time, though, love bears all things (1 Cor. 13:7a). This verse doesn't mean that love overlooks sin in people's lives. Rather, it means love puts a roof over someone. Dr. Wayne Mack explains the concept that love "bears" all things when he writes:

> The verb Paul uses here can also mean "to cover or protect." Used in its noun form in Mark 2:4, it is translated by the word "roof." . . . The "roof" is there to protect the home from the elements. It also serves to keep people from seeing inside the house. Therefore, it functions as a means of protection . . . . The verb form of the word used in 1 Corinthians 13:7, according to the Greek dictionary, can literally mean "to put a roof over what is displeasing in another person," "to throw a cloak of silence over what is displeasing in another person," "to pass over in silence or to keep confidential or to protect and preserve by covering." In other words, it means to cover over with silence, to keep secret, to hide or conceal the errors and faults of others.[27]

So, love does not merely overlook sin, nor does it allow someone to remain in her habitual sin. Rather, love protects another by protecting her from harmful exposure due to her sin. At the same time, love helps another put off her sin and put on the righteous alternative. We can only truly begin to deal biblically with our sin when we are willing to expose it for what it is and work at replacing it with behaviors and thoughts that please the Lord. This kind of growth from freedom of honest expression won't happen if one fears judgment or condemnation from the other person.

What are some of the hard things that Barbara has had to say

27   Wayne A. Mack, *Maximum Impact*, (Phillipsburg, NJ: P&R Publishing Company, 2010), 214. Dr. Mack's definition comes from *A Greek English Lexicon of the New Testament*, ed. William Arndt et al. (Chicago, IL: University of Chicago Press, 1957), 772; W. E. Vine, *Vine's Complete Expository Dictionary of Old and New Testament Words* (Nashville, TN: Thomas Nelson, 1996), 53.

to me in love? There are so many examples to choose from that I have had to narrow down the list quite a bit! An early example took place over fifteen years ago, shortly after Craig and I finished our marriage counseling. In this incident, Craig had made a decision that would have caused me embarrassment. In tears, I called Barbara to tell her that Craig wanted to cancel our son's birthday party due to a discipline issue with him. This cancellation was going to occur after the invitations had gone out to all the boys in Andrew's first-grade class. After listening to the whole story, Barbara asked me some questions to get to the heart of the issue. She asked, "Didn't you want your husband to step up and lead? If so, then, why do you not want him to do it?" Basically, she was asking me why I was not submitting to his headship. Then she asked me to call Craig and explain to him how I was wrong to question his parenting decision and to tell him that I wanted him to lead in the discipline of the children no matter what. By the time I was able to reach Craig to communicate all of this to him, Andrew had repented and the party went on without a hitch.

Another example involved only me. During a time of fasting and praying at our church, I realized that my desire for my children's obedience had become an idol in my heart. An idol of the heart is *"anything that rules me other than God."*[28] I knew this good desire had become an idol because I vacillated between anger to get their obedience and despair when I couldn't make them obey. My good desire had become idolatrous when it became an inordinate desire.

I told Barbara I realized that I must have my children obey; I will have my children obey. Barbara asked me to look up Isaiah 14 and read verses 12–14. She then told me I was manifesting attributes of Satan. Now, before you gasp, hear me out: she didn't stop there! While she actually used those words with me, she went on to explain how I was trying to make myself like God in this way, as Satan had. Satan wanted to be like the Most High God (Isa. 14:14). He wanted to be the Sovereign Ruler, the One with all control. This was who I was trying to be to my children. Barbara warned me of the dangers of setting up an idol of control in my heart and allowing it to remain there (Ezek. 14: 1–8). She

28   Paul David Tripp, *Instruments In The Redeemer's Hands: People In Need Of Change Helping People In Need of Change* (Phillipsburg, NJ: P&R Publishing Company, 2002), 66.

went on to tell me that she didn't want this for me and that she was confident that I didn't want to behave this way or compete with God in such a way. Barbara began to instruct me in how to put off this sin and she helped me do it (and continues to do so to this day when it creeps up in my heart). Only someone who loves another and fears God would have the courage to say what Barbara had to say to me that day. Barbara didn't count the cost to herself; she didn't wonder if it would cause me never to speak to her again. She said what she needed to say in a kind way and what would best benefit me. On the other hand, I knew she cared about me and was telling me the truth. Even though it was hard to hear, I humbled myself and began in earnest to put off this idol of control.

I'm choosing the next example because it highlights the importance of speaking a hard and honest truth no matter the situation; it highlights that we can't let a painful situation be an excuse to not say what needs to be said. While I understand that we need to "weep with those who weep" (Rom. 12:15) and be sensitive to one another's pain, true friends speak freely to one another without fear of rejection.

In March of 2011, my family moved my grandmother, Nan, into our house after Nan had spent some time recovering in a rehabilitation facility. Everyone was looking forward to cooking with Nan each night. However, she had to go back to rehab again. The day before Easter, I had gone to visit her. On the way home, I bought vegetable seeds and proceeded to plant them in the garden. Although I had gotten them in late, I was especially excited about the prospect of making sauce with Nan from the tomatoes I would eventually harvest. Instead, I received a call from a nurse around 5:00 a.m. Easter morning. Nan had died in her sleep. Barbara mourned the loss of Nan with me.

A few months after Nan's passing, I was gazing out the window, looking at the tomato plants. I commented to Barbara that I would not be able to make sauce with my grandmother as I had planned. Barbara gently told me to think about all the things I had gotten to do with my grandmother, to think on those things rather than the one thing I wouldn't be able to do. She also warned me to be careful of accusing God of wrongdoing in His sovereign timing of Nan's death. Barbara encouraged me to focus instead on how much I had to be thankful for by telling me to make a "thankful list." A thankful list is merely a list enumerating all the things for which we can be thankful. For instance, I listed the blessing that Nan had lived a full life of eighty-nine years. Next, I wrote that I was able to enjoy our relationship for forty-two years. Moreover, I thanked God that my children had had an opportunity to develop a relationship with their great-grandmother. And the list could go on and on. The point is that Barbara wanted me to be thankful in all things (1 Thess. 5:18). Just those small changes in thinking helped me significantly in dealing with my unexpected loss in the days, weeks, and months that followed.

As I mentioned earlier, there are many examples that I could use to illustrate the vital importance of having a relationship that communicates freely and honestly. Barbara once had to help me put on tenderhearted thoughts toward a meter man who struck my dog on the flank and in the eye in front of the children. While my dog, Amber, thought she was protecting Lauren and Andrew, the man probably thought he was saving his own life. Barbara wanted me to give the meter man the benefit of the doubt because Amber was a big yellow lab with a scary bark (although she never bit anyone in her fourteen years). Barbara was able to give the man the benefit of the doubt and counsel me to do the same in my thoughts of him and what he had done because she wasn't as emotionally involved in the incident as I was. This principle will prove to be true in any discipleship relationship: the one who is less emotional will be able to think more biblically and give wiser counsel. I could also share how Barbara once admonished me when I was being critical of Craig for bringing grass clippings into the garage after he had mowed the grass. Why would I think no grass would be on the underside of the mower? It should also be mentioned that I had previously instructed Craig on the best pattern to mow the grass. But that's another story!

Another way that Barbara and I have grown together in Christ is how we have encouraged each other's giftedness. First of all, Barbara used some of her resources to help me get Precept training and study aids so that I could foster my gift of teaching. She also paid for me to go to conferences to help me hone my skills as a counselor. We spent (and still spend) time discussing lessons as we prepare to teach them, determining not only what is most important to say but also the best way to communicate those truths to our audience. After a lesson, we discuss how we thought it went, ways in which we could improve it, and things that we did well. For instance, when teaching, I have a tendency to be extremely intense. While some may view this trait as passion, it can appear harsh during a lesson. Barbara came up with a signal to help me recognize the times that I'm coming across that way when I'm teaching so that I can "turn it down a notch." We would never want the person's tone of voice to get in the way of someone hearing what God has to say. Again, none of this is to bring the other down; rather, it's just the opposite: we are trying to help one another in our teaching of the Word since we are ultimately held responsible by God to handle His Word accurately (2 Tim. 2:15). This awareness of our delivery helps us keep a high view of God's Word ourselves.

All these examples highlight Solomon's perspective in Ecclesiastes 4:9–12 where he states:

> Two are better than one because they have a good return for their labor. For if either of them falls, the one will lift up his companion. But woe to the one who falls when there is not another to lift him up. Furthermore, if two lie down together they keep warm, but how can one be warm alone? And if one can overpower him who is alone, two can resist him. A cord of three strands is not quickly torn apart.

Solomon's instruction in Ecclesiastes has proven to be true in my relationship with Barbara. Two are indeed better than one. We are firmly convinced that we have had a "good return," a better return because we have labored to grow in Christ together. Believers need one another. They are interdependent. Believers were never meant to be "lone rangers." Sanctification occurs ideally in community as believers strive to practice all of the one-another passages in Scripture (Heb. 10:23–24). In fact, the next chapter will include further ways that we continue to grow together.

For now, I hope you see more clearly the importance of believing the best of one another so that God's Word can be rightly applied to the life of a disciple and friend. I hope you see how, in all things, we must speak an applicable word to one another, no matter what the situation, if we desire growth in the other person. Usually, it's in the hard things of life where we need the most help. The hard things involve all kinds of situations, ranging from spouses and death, at the one end, to the mundane like yard work and even dealing with our pets, at the other. I also hope that you noted what we did to invest in the relationship, particularly in fostering the giftedness of each other and how those practices distinguish this type of relationship from a mere friendship. I hope I have given you encouragement to "walk in a manner worthy of [your] calling" and to help others do so as well along the journey (Eph. 4:1).

For Further Thought

....

1. Is there a woman in whom you recognize the gift of teaching who can instruct you?

2. Is there a woman you've noticed who is as eager a learner as Gina was?

3. Is there a woman whom you can talk freely with, who would not be appalled at your sin?

4. Is there a woman who would not judge you for your sin nor help you justify your sin, but rather, would help you put it off?

5. Are you willing to say truthful things even when they are hard in order to help a friend?

6. Is there any way you can encourage others' giftedness? If so, how can you do this practically?

7. Since two are better than one according to Ecclesiastes 4:9, who could enhance your fruitfulness?

7

Sustained Growth for the Journey

[L]et us consider how to stimulate one another to love and good deeds, not forsaking our own assembling together, as is the habit of some, but encouraging one another; and all the more as you see the day drawing near.
(Hebrews 10:24–25)

• • • • • • • • • • • • • •

We highlighted some of the unique ways that we helped each other mature in Christ together in our last chapter. However, our growth was not limited to just teaching through admonishment, being honest and confessing our sins to each other, putting a roof over each other, and encouraging each other's giftedness. Let's go back to our example of gardening. The novice gardener focuses on a few primary and fundamental aspects of gardening in order to begin her garden. However, the seasoned gardener focuses on the nuances of gardening to enhance the growth of the plants. For example, vegetables from the cabbage family will actually produce a greater yield if they are grown together with members from the green, leafy vegetable family or along with beets. Or, you might have heard that certain plants ward off certain bugs. For instance, marigolds are a natural insecticide for tomato plants, repelling tomato hornworms which are known to attack tomato plants. Interestingly, what we've just described is called companion planting. If this kind of knowledge is necessary for a vegetable garden, how much more is this true for sustaining and enhancing spiritual growth!

Sustained Growth

What are some other ways that we sustained our spiritual growth? Gina and I also grew together by practicing all of the "one-another" passages that are found in the Bible. One of our favorite Bible studies is to do a study of each of these particular passages. Depending upon how you group them, there are at least fifty-nine different commands in the New Testament which state how we are to treat one another and relate to one another. We are instructed to put into practice the teachings found in these passages in our conduct toward other believers, but we also need others to "one-another" us. The most frequently repeated "one-another" command, however, is that we are to "love one another."[29]

There are many words that the Bible translates as *love* in the New Testament. One of the words is from the Greek word *philéō*, which is a love with the "meaning of having common interests with another."[30] *Philadelphía* speaks of "the love of Christians one to another, brotherly love, out of a common spiritual life."[31] These words imply more of a familial, affectionate love. In Titus 2:4 older women are told to "encourage the young women to love their husbands, to love their children." Both of the words *love* used in this verse are a form of the word *philéō*. This word is also used in the context of Christians having a brotherly love and affection toward one another. Paul ends his letter to Titus by writing, "All who are with me greet you. Greet those who love [*philéō*] us in the faith. Grace be with you all" (Titus 3:15).

Another word in the New Testament for *love* is from the Greek word *agápē*. This word is translated *charity* in the King James Version of the Bible and it implies a benevolent love. "Its benevolence, however, is not shown by doing what the person loved desires but what the one who loves deems as needed by the one loved."[32] As an illustration, "God so loved the world that He gave . . ." (John 3:16a). What did He give? Not what man desired, but what God deemed man needed—His only begotten Son, Jesus Christ.

This concept of love is crucial to our understanding of the holy love of God. Too often, when people are asked to describe God's love, they reply, "God's love is unconditional." This description can be misleading. This answer implies that God's love is a fluffy, non-restrictive kind of love. While it is true that God's love can never fail, that truth does not mean that His love caters to our every desire and demand. His love gives us what He deems is best for us, not what we think we need. It is not a "whatever-you-want" kind of love.

---

29 For example see John 13:34–35; Romans 13:8–10; and 1 Peter 4:8.
30 Zodhiates, *Key Study Bible*, 1885.
31 Ibid., 1885.
32 Ibid., 1796.

First Thessalonians 4:9 uses a form of both words *philéō* and *agápē*. "Now as to the love [*philadelphía*] of the brethren, you have no need for anyone to write to you, for you yourselves are taught by God to love [*agapáō*] one another." Gina and I grew in our understanding of what it really means to love one another. While our affection for each other grew over the years, we believe that the crucial element that pushed us forward in our sanctification was *agape* love. We made progress in sanctification when we came to understand that. Have you ever heard someone say, "We just need to love her" in response to hearing that a person is in sin? We have! For example, you may have a friend who has a habit of gossiping. Almost every time she is in a group of ladies, she finds a way to speak ill of someone. You seek counsel from another friend on how to best handle the situation and she says, "We just need to love her." Here is the problem. Love does not leave a person in sin. When God set His love on His children, He rescued them from the penalty of sin, the power of sin, and, eventually, He will rescue us from the presence of sin. The point is this: God's love does not leave us in our sin! So, if we want to truly love (*agape*) one another, we should help one another forsake sin.

Gina and I have learned to do just that. We do not remain silent when the other one is in sin. Rather, we rebuke each other because we love (*agape*) each other. We give what we deem is necessary and best for the other person. I can remember once when I was "venting" over the phone with Gina about an upset. Gina knew that expressing such emotions was wrong based on Proverbs 29:11 which says, "A fool gives full vent to his spirit, but a wise man quietly holds it back" (ESV). Even so, she quipped, "You are angry and venting." "But it is all right because it is just me." I replied. "No, it is not all right because venting is not a biblical practice and goes against Ephesians 4:29 which says, 'Let no unwholesome word proceed from your mouth, but only such a word as is good for edification according to the need of the moment, so that it will give grace to those who hear.'" Gina and I have learned to say to each other, "Don't help me justify my sin. Please don't help me excuse my sinful behavior." Instead, we have the freedom to stop each other when the other one is practicing sinful communication and then we encourage each other to use

God-honoring speech. This is just one small example of how we strive to love each other, not unconditionally, but by giving to the one being loved what she needs.

Another "one-another" command that we try to practice and which has helped to sustain our growth in Christ is found in Romans 12:10. In this verse, Paul writes that we are to be "devoted to one another in brotherly love; give preference to one another in honor." In other words, we are to be devoted, to be committed in our love for one another just as one would a family member. We are to prefer one another and try to outdo the other person in honoring him or her. We must not insist upon having our own way, but we should lead the way in honoring the other person's preference. I will illustrate this with one small example of how Gina puts this into practice. It happens when we go out to eat together and share a steak. Gina agrees to order the steak cooked medium well. While it may seem like a small thing, you have to remember how Gina feels about food! However, she is willing to put aside her preferences for a properly cooked steak (which is medium rare, by the way) to show preference to me in this matter. On the flip side, I reciprocate by allowing Gina to drive even though I enjoy driving. I do this because I know that Gina has a tendency to get motion sickness. I even let Gina drive me through the traffic in Los Angeles as I held on for dear life! Again, it's a small thing; but it highlights how we both try to outdo honoring the other by not insisting on having our own selfish preferences.

While I have mentioned just two of the many "one-another" passages, Gina and I aim, although imperfectly, to practice all of them. More importantly, we highly encourage all our readers to do a study. We have provided in the appendix a study written by Dr. Wayne Mack. This is the study we have done together and use often in our counseling. We prefer his study because he challenges believers to think of ways to actually implement what the Bible commands us to do.[33] We think you'll find it helpful as you seek to "one-another" those around you and allow yourself to be "one-anothered."

While we continued to practice the "one-anothering" passages, we also sustained our growth in Christ by growing in

---

33   See Appendix B for this homework.

our knowledge of doctrine. Gina and I were blessed to attend a church where sound theology was expounded from the pulpit by our pastor. He preached expositorily through the Bible. His faithful exposition of the Word prevented him from doing topical Bible teaching which allows some preachers to simply ride their "hobby horses." In other words, as he preached verse by verse through various books of the Bible, it enabled him to preach the whole counsel of God, not just his favorite topics (Acts 20:27). Second Timothy 4:3–4 states: "For the time will come when they will not endure sound doctrine; but wanting to have their ears tickled, they will accumulate for themselves teachers in accordance to their own desires, and will turn away their ears from the truth and will turn aside to myths." Because our pastor taught expositorily, our ears were not "tickled." Moreover, we were taught sound doctrine which enabled us to grow in our knowledge of God, the gospel, sanctification, and redemption. Really, we grew in all of God's truth.

Another way that God used this man to help us grow in our knowledge of doctrine was through the classes in systematic theology he held for his congregation. We studied many theological issues which ranged from creation to eschatology. This class afforded Gina and me an opportunity to hammer out some of our own personal convictions on the deeper theological issues. It grieves us to this day when we hear some women say that they don't want to study theology. We don't think they realize what they are actually saying. Theology is merely the study of God. The word theology comes from the "Greek words *theos* (God) and *logos* (word) which suggest the 'word concerning God' or 'the study of God.' "[34] So, you see why it grieves us to hear believers say that they don't want to study theology. What Christian would not want to study her God! In fact, growing in our knowledge of God helped us not only personally but also as we taught and counseled other women.

While at Grace Bible Church, Gina and I studied many books of the Bible with the use of Precept workbooks. The ladies were taught how to study the Bible inductively. What does it mean to study the Bible inductively? Kay Arthur explains it this way:

---

34   Rolland McCune, *A Systematic Theology of Biblical Christianity*, vol. 1 (Allen Park, MI: Detroit Baptist Theological Seminary, 2009), 3.

"Inductive study doesn't tell you what the Bible means or what you should believe. Instead, it teaches you a method of studying God's Word that can be applied to any portion of Scripture at any time for the rest of your life."[35] This method includes observing the biblical text, interpreting the text, and then applying the text. After studying biblical counseling, however, I added a fourth step which I call implementing the text. As one labors to determine the meaning of the text based on observation, she receives meat, not milk (Heb. 5:12–13). John Bunyan put it eloquently when he stated:

> Although you may have no commentaries at hand, continue to read the Word and pray; for a little from God is better than a great deal received from a man. Too many are content to listen to what comes from men's mouths, without searching and kneeling before God to know the real truth. That which we receive directly from the Lord through the study of His Word is from the minting house itself. Even old truths are new if they come to us with the smell of heaven upon them.[36]

Through inductive studying, Gina and I learned, and continue to learn, the Bible in context rather than piecemeal. This method of studying affords us a high view of God and His Word.

While teaching the Bible inductively at Grace Bible Church, I often had women come to me to discuss problems they were experiencing. While I was able to empathize with these women, I often felt as if I had no concrete answers for the problems that they faced. I could give them vague biblical counsel such as "Trust God," "God is sovereign," or "Pray about the situation." While those statements are true, they did not provide the women with practical ways in which those truths could be applied.

In God's providence, He sent me to The Master's University where I was able to study biblical counseling under the instruction of many godly men. One of those men was one of the leaders in the biblical counseling movement, Dr. Wayne Mack. It was under the teaching of Dr. Mack that I clearly understood that the

---

35   Kay Arthur, *How To Study Your Bible* (Eugene, OR: Harvest House Publishers, 1994), 7.
36   As quoted by Doug McIntosh, *God Up Close* (Chicago, IL: Moody Press, 1998), 84.

Scriptures are truly sufficient.[37] While many evangelicals claim to believe in the sufficiency of Scripture, Dr. Mack expounds it, counsels it, and lives it. He believes the Bible is sufficient because the Bible claims to be sufficient. He also demonstrates that he believes in the sufficiency of the Scriptures because he does not integrate psychological concepts with his counseling. As I studied biblical counseling under Dr. Mack and other godly instructors, Gina was able to read many of the books that I was required to read and she also read most of the papers that I was required to write. We had many opportunities to discuss how to apply our biblical knowledge to the practical matters of daily life.

It was through studying biblical counseling together that rapid growth took place. Biblical counseling taught Gina and me how to take our "formal" theology and turn it into our "functional" theology. In other words, biblical counseling taught us how to implement the biblical knowledge that we had gained. For instance, we know that we are commanded by our Lord in Matthew 6 not to worry or be anxious. So, how does biblical counseling translate that knowledge into action? First, we learned to repent of the sin of worry. It is not someone's fixed temperament or situation that causes her to worry. Then we learned how to replace worry and anxiety with the righteous alternative which is trusting God. From this particular passage, God tells us that anxiety comes from serving two masters (Matt. 6:19–24). God reminds us to consider the birds of the air and the lilies of the field in order to increase our faith. Our Heavenly Father knows what we need and He will provide because He is faithful. If He provides for them, how much more will He provide for His children. Christ ends His teaching by reminding us of what is important: seeking His Kingdom and His righteousness first. He promises that when we are obedient in these ways, all things necessary will be added to us. As we disciplined ourselves to think on these things rather than trying to serve two masters, we were able to put off our worry and put on a robust trust in God. This is just one example of how biblical counseling helped us put

---

37 For a thorough discussion on the positions of the biblical counseling movement read *Counseling: How to Counsel Biblically* by John MacArthur, Dr. Wayne Mack, and other members of The Master's University Faculty published by Thomas Nelson, Inc., 2005.

"feet" to our theological knowledge, helping us mature in Christ.

Gina and I were able to sustain our growth in Christ not only by studying theology, and not only by studying the Bible inductively, but also by studying biblical counseling together. These additional disciplines and practices are like the companion planting we mentioned at the beginning of the chapter. They enhanced our growth in Christ along the journey.

For Further Thought
....

1. If you haven't done so already, complete the study on the "one-anothering" passages found in Appendix B.

2. Consider Proverbs 27:5–6 which states: "Better is open rebuke Than love that is concealed. Faithful are the wounds of a friend, But deceitful are the kisses of an enemy." How do these verses relate to the definition of *agápē* as given in this chapter?

3. As you think about your closest sisters in Christ, are you being a faithful friend by rebuking your friends when they are caught in a habitual sin?

4. How would you rate yourself when it comes to showing preference to those in your life: your family, your church (Rom. 12:10)?

5. Consider Philippians 2:3–4 which states: "Do nothing from selfishness or empty conceit, but with humility of mind regard one another as more important than yourselves; do not merely look out for your own personal interests, but also for the interests of others." How do these verses relate to the admonition to prefer one another?

6. For at least one day (trying this for a week would be better!), list the times you do not assert your own interests, even in small ways.

7. While we are not encouraging you to complain against the leadership of your church, are you truly getting sound doctrine from the pulpit or are you having your ears tickled (2 Tim. 4:3–4)?

8. To help you grow in understanding theology, we would recommend the following books for study. While not everyone would agree with every theological point, we have found Wayne Grudem's *Systematic Theology* to be the most reader friendly. You could also go through Louis Berkhof's *Systematic Theology* or Bruce Milne's *Know the Truth* to help you in your pursuit of growing in your theological knowledge.

There is also a theology book, edited by John MacArthur and Richard Mayhue. Its title is *Biblical Doctrine*.

9. Other resources to help you grow in your knowledge of the attributes of God include *Knowing God* by J. I. Packer, *The Attributes of God* by A. W. Pink, and *The Knowledge of the Holy* by A. W. Tozer.

10. We cannot stress enough the importance of studying the Bible inductively. If you are not already involved in a study at your local church, go to www.precept.org to find a Precept study in your area.

11. Since we all give and receive counsel every day, evaluate the type of counsel that you give and receive. Does it reflect the sufficiency of Scripture, that God has given us all things necessary for life and godliness (2 Peter 1:3)? If not, consider using the following resources to begin thinking more biblically about what causes man's behavior (your behavior). We recommend *Counseling: How to Counsel Biblically* by John MacArthur, Dr. Wayne Mack, and the faculty of The Master's University; *Instruments in the Redeemer's Hands: People in Need of Change Helping People in Need of Change* by Paul David Tripp; and *Women Counseling Women: Biblical Answers to Life's Difficult Problems* edited by Elyse Fitzpatrick. (By the way, Barbara wrote a chapter on hermeneutics for that book.)

8

A Needful Warning
for the Journey

For anyone of the house of Israel or of the immigrants who stay in Israel who separates himself from Me, sets up his idols in his heart, puts right before his face the stumbling block of his iniquity, and then comes to the prophet to inquire of Me for himself, I the LORD will be brought to answer him in My own person.
(Ezekiel 14:7)

• • • • • • • • • • •

We all know the account of creation when God created the world from nothing. As God was creating day by day, the repeated refrain is heard, "God saw that it was good." Then we come across these stunning words: something was not good! What could possibly be considered *not good*? We read God's declaration. "Then the LORD God said, 'It is not good for the man to be alone' . . ." (Gen. 2:18). Man is a relational being and should not live in isolation. In fact, part of being an image-bearer of God is that man was created for relationships.

Biblical Relationships

The Scriptures define relationships and teach how relationships should be developed and maintained. In order to determine accurately what a relationship is, one must turn to the wisdom of the Creator of relationships. The Creator God has eternally existed in a perfect relationship of three Persons in One, which theologians call the Trinity. Looking at the Trinity, one can see that a relationship is the intimate involvement of two or more persons interacting within a union of cherished knowledge and enjoyment of one another. One biblical scholar writes of the unique and glorious relationship of the Triune God. He states:

> The Trinity is a relationship in which three eternal persons (each being perfect in character and totally equal in being, power, and glory) reveal, know, and love each other tenderly and perfectly for the other's good within the context of an eternal commitment. When they decide to set and accom-

plish a goal, for the purpose of order and economy, God the Son and God the Spirit voluntarily subordinate themselves to God the Father in order to function according to their perfect plans. As they work together, they are totally unified in desire, thought and action until the goal's completion. Thus, they are a plurality within a unity.[38]

The Triune God, totally satisfied in an eternally perfect relationship, has given us specific directions concerning how to relate to one another. So, we know He takes our horizontal relationships seriously. Our human relationships should, therefore, be patterned after the Trinity.

As is our sinful tendency, we take a gracious gift of God and twist it into something He never intended. Consider, for instance, food. God could have sustained us with something akin to manna, but instead He provided fruits and various types of grains and veggies. We have so many different types, flavors, and textures to enjoy. But what have we done with His plentiful gifts? Our sinful propensity is to abuse those gifts. In other words, we've taken what He's provided for our benefit and pleasure and used it in a way He never intended. As an example, every time we are enjoying a particular meal to the point of gluttony, we are abusing God's gracious gift of food. We are not eating for the glory of God, giving Him thanks for what's in front of us (1 Cor. 10:31). Thus, we are sinning. We are using the food to satisfy some desire or lust in our hearts and definitely not exercising self-control, which is one manifestation of the fruit of the Spirit (Gal. 5:22–23). The abuse of God's gracious gift can be the same with the discipleship relationship.

Let me explain. In His kindness, God provided a wise woman to come alongside me to help me grow in Christlikeness. However, for a time, Barbara was my idol. It was not that I was worshipping her, but I had put my hope and trust in her. I sincerely believed that if anything happened to her, I could not live or I would not know how to live without her. At the time, in the early stages of our relationship, I didn't know it was happening. It wasn't like either of us was purposefully sinning. I don't even think Barbara

38   Stuart Scott as quoted by Martha Peace, *The Excellent Wife* (Bemidji, MN: Focus Publishing, Inc., 1999), 30.

was aware of my perspective (indeed, she was not). Nonetheless, it was sin on my part. I'm sure you've heard it said that even if you don't know the speed limit but you're caught speeding, you're still guilty of breaking the law. The same principle applies here.

But, looking back, I can see clearly how it happened. Because God will not share His glory with another (Isa. 42:8), Barbara and I wanted to include this chapter in our book. Idols are a serious offense against our holy God (Ezek. 14:1–8). Moreover, because heart idolatry is also foolish, destructive, and deceptive (Ps. 115:3–8), we want to help you avoid this sin as you pursue your discipleship relationship. John Piper writes of the subtle deceptiveness of heart idolatry:

> The greatest enemy of hunger for God is not poison but apple pie. It is not the banquet of the wicked that dulls our appetite for heaven, but endless nibbling at the table of the world. It is not the X-rated video, but the prime-time dribble of triviality we drink in every night. For all the ill that Satan can do, when God describes what keeps us from the banquet table of his love, it is a piece of land, a yoke of oxen, and a wife (Luke 14:18–20). The greatest adversary of love to God is not his enemies, but his gifts. And the most deadly appetites are not for the poison of evil, but for the simple pleasures of earth. For when these replace an appetite for God himself, the idolatry is scarcely recognizable, and almost incurable.[39]

The thing that makes heart idolatry so deceptive and "scarcely recognizable and almost incurable" is when a good desire becomes an inordinate desire. An inordinate desire is one that is out of order or exceeds reasonable limits. It was not wrong for me to desire a discipleship relationship with Barbara. But the problem was it replaced what should have been my first desire—a desire to know Christ.

One of the things that contributed to my setting up Barbara as an idol in my heart was my marriage relationship. I want to be careful in describing how Craig and I *used* to operate. While we knew the husband was the head of the wife/family and the wife

---

39   John Piper, *A Hunger For God* (Wheaton, IL: Crossway Books, 1997), 14.

was to submit to the husband, we really didn't know what that looked like practically. This was a time period in our marriage before we received biblical counseling. This is also an example of what Barbara and I were discussing in the last chapter, namely, knowing a biblical truth but not understanding how to implement it. Functioning in this unbiblical way was due partly to ignorance and partly to receiving and believing bad counsel. Bottom line, it was all sin. As I said, Craig and I providentially received biblical counseling and presently enjoy a oneness that I never thought possible.

However, at the time, I did not hold him in the esteem that the Bible calls a wife to have toward her husband. As a result, I did not talk to him about spiritual things in as much depth or as frequently as I did with Barbara. Since he and I weren't communicating biblically, when we did try to have discussions, we oftentimes wound up in conflict rather than delighting in understanding each other (Prov. 18:2). I started saying things like, "Barbara said ..." to support my opinion. I'm sure he thought (rightly so) that my allegiance was to her rather than to him where it should have been. Even if Craig was theologically wrong or he and I differed on some minute point, I should have communicated honor and respect to him in my words and actions. I also contributed to the problem by being what Martha Peace calls a "truth monster." I was a noisy gong since I didn't exercise care to ensure that my words were seasoned with grace (1 Cor. 13:1; Col. 4:6). I regret to say that my husband was the one who took the brunt of my sinfulness.

Another way I favored Barbara over Craig was that I did not greet him when he came home. Usually, I was on the phone with Barbara while cooking dinner. This repeated action must have communicated to him that he was an interruption to my day and my agenda. When my spouse walked through the door after being away most of the day, I should have greeted him warmly. A kind, intentional greeting would have communicated that I was glad to have him home. More importantly, it would have demonstrated that he was so significant to me that I was willing to stop what I was doing for a few brief moments to acknowledge his presence. Greeting your husband when he comes home communicates respect to him and is one way to demonstrate that he is your primary ministry.[40]

Moreover, I had jealousy in my heart when Barbara had to minister to others, whether it was her daughter or another woman. I would have never admitted it, nor did I get mad at her and hold a grudge. In fact, I knew I was wrong. But I can recall being inwardly upset if Barbara and I didn't get to sit together at women's events because then I couldn't talk to her the way I wanted to. I actually even referred to her for a time as "my Barbara," as if I couldn't share her friendship with anyone else. I can't imagine how childish that must have come across to people.

When God says that we are not to have other gods before Him, nor set up idols, He means it (Ex. 20:3–4). As John Calvin has said, our hearts are a "perpetual factory of idols."[41] Jeremiah warns us concerning putting our trust in another person. In Jeremiah 17:5–6 we read:

> Thus says the LORD,
> "Cursed is the man who trusts in mankind
> And makes flesh his strength,
> And whose heart turns away from the LORD.
> For he will be like a bush in the desert
> And will not see when prosperity comes,
> But will live in stony wastes in the wilderness,
> A land of salt without inhabitant."

In setting up Barbara as my idol, I did not realize at the time that I was also turning away from the Lord in my heart.

God, as always and as usual, was gracious to me. The first way He revealed this idol to me was by showing me that I was depending on Barbara too much for too many things. For instance, I expected her to be omnipresent in that if I needed her I expected her to be always available. Moreover, I was trusting in her to be my refuge which is contrary to Psalm 46:1 which teaches us that "God is our refuge and strength, A very present help in trouble."

---

40   To get a thorough and biblical view on the role of the Christian wife, we highly recommend Martha Peace's book, *The Excellent Wife*, cited previously in this chapter.

41   John Calvin, *Institutes of the Christian Religion*, ed. John T. McNeill, 2 vols., Library of Christian Classics (Philadelphia, PA: Westminster Press, 1960), 1:108.

God is the only One that can always be available. He taught me this truth incrementally.

The first time I thought I was losing Barbara was when she moved further away from me. Ironically, she moved only about fifteen minutes further away than she had been before. Nonetheless, I was convinced that we wouldn't be friends anymore because of her move. This irrational fear highlights how I was making Barbara my refuge, my idol. Nothing between us really changed at that time, so I didn't have to deal with my idolatrous heart.

Then she went to the Master's University to work on her MABC. This commitment meant she would be gone for a few weeks in the summer and be in classes. We'd be on different time schedules, and I wouldn't be able to talk to her whenever I needed to. Two things happened to help me. First, I was forced to turn to the Lord. I know that sounds funny when we've been saying for seven chapters that a discipleship relationship needs to be built on pursuing Christ. So, you would think that I was regularly depending on the Lord and not another human being. That's what I meant earlier when I said that this dependency happened subtly and Barbara probably wasn't aware of it. The subtleness of idolatry is just an example of the deceitfulness of sin. As believers we are interdependent and we still need counsel from one another. But the point is we are to seek the Lord first before running to a close friend. So, even though I was not fully aware of my idolatrous emotional attachment, the Lord was faithful to deal with my heart in His time. As I began to turn to Him in loneliness or with unresolved questions, He showed Himself to be an ever-present help; I was never alone. Moreover, Christ was a sympathetic High Priest (Heb. 4:14–16). He, more than anyone, even Barbara, understood perfectly everything I was going through at any given time. He was never too busy or out of town; He never misunderstood. He always welcomed me and, in fact, beckoned me to come (Matt. 11:28–30). As I meditated on these two truths, I began to turn away from my idol.

The second thing that helped me during this time happened late in the first week Barbara was gone to college. She was able to call me one evening after classes and one of the first statements that came out of her mouth was, "I couldn't wait to talk to you!" It was at this point that I realized that neither distance nor her pursuing her biblical counseling degree would change our relationship. All the other people she was going to class with, the new friends she was making wouldn't change our love for each other. God allowed Barbara to say those words to me that particular night in order to communicate her love for me. He didn't have to do that.

Due to some relationships as a result of her going to The Master's University, Barbara planned to visit South Africa with her husband. I panicked. She was going to be gone for weeks. How would I survive without talking to her? I really thought she was going to die on the plane trip over the Atlantic and I would not be able to live without her. Who would help me if I had a problem? Who would listen to me? Counsel me? Accept me? I had so much to learn! As you can see, my idol was not yet fully torn down.

I don't know how it happened, but I came across the book *Damsels in Distress* by Martha Peace. Martha has a chapter entitled "What Do You Mean I Can Live Without Him? Idolatrous Emotional Attachments."[42] While you might not be familiar with that terminology, I bet you've heard phrases such as co-dependent or enabler. Well, those are just psychological terms for not relating biblically to one another or having another person be an idol in your heart, which is what I had allowed Barbara to become. Instead of saying I can't live without Christ, I said (in my heart) I can't live without Barbara. Through reading that chapter and recognizing the fear that was going on in my heart, I realized the extent of my idolatry and repented. I began to ask God to give me a heart that desired *Him* above all else, that couldn't live without *Him,* that if He chose to take Barbara away, I could go on serving Him as long as I had Him.

I was able to teach Martha's book to the women at our church in the summer of 2011. I remember describing how I had set Barbara up in my heart as an idol. It was hard to admit. I was also able to tell the women that when, by God's grace, I put God in His rightful place in my heart, my relationship with Barbara got even better. Who would have thought? But it's true. And why should we be surprised. The principle is that when we are operating

---

42   Peace, *Damsels In Distress,* 45–57.

according to biblical guidelines, no matter what those guidelines are, we enjoy more freedom, more benefits. Psalm 119:45 says, "I will walk at liberty, For I seek Your precepts." He created us after all and knows what's best for us. God promises blessing and fruitfulness when we put our trust in Him. God tells us this truth in Jeremiah 17:7–8 where we read:

> Blessed is the man who trusts in the LORD
> And whose trust is the LORD.
> For he will be like a tree planted by the water,
> That extends its roots by a stream
> And will not fear when the heat comes;
> But its leaves will be green,
> And it will not be anxious in a year of drought
> Nor cease to yield fruit.

No longer do I have any jealousy about any of Barbara's other relationships. No longer am I upset if we don't get to sit together at women's events. In fact, we actually try not to sit together so that we can minister to other women. Now I no longer wonder if she really wants to speak with me. Most importantly, even though I would hate to have to live without Barbara, I know I could if the Lord chooses to call her home before me.

While I am thankful for the gracious gift of my discipleship relationship with Barbara, I am even more grateful that God exposed how I was misusing this relationship. I am thankful that God turned my heart from trusting in "man" and turned it toward trusting in the Lord. While this chapter was hard to write, it is a necessary warning against the danger of making "flesh and blood" your refuge as you journey in your discipleship relationship.

For Further Thought

1. Meditate on the beauty of the relationship that exists among the Persons of the Trinity as set forth in the beginning of this chapter by Stuart Scott. Write down the various aspects of their union and how it should apply to our relationships.

2. Since the relationship of the Trinity is the perfect pattern for human relationships, examine your closest relationships in light of this pattern. How do your closest relationships measure up? Is there anything you need to change?

3. Are there ways that you have taken God's gracious gift of friendship and turned it into a sinful relationship?

4. Read Ezekiel 14:1–8 to capture the seriousness of setting up idols in your heart. Write down the specific consequences God gives for setting up these idols. Based on the passage, what is God's solution to setting up idols in your heart?

5. Read Jeremiah 17:5–6. Make a specific list of what happens to the man (or woman) who trusts in mankind. Drawing a picture of this person will be a helpful visual aid.

6. Although we want to be able to trust a faithful friend, there is only one Person whom we can trust 100 percent: God Himself! How has trusting in a person, expecting him or her to be what only God can be brought you disappointment? Can you see the futility of that sin?

7. Read Jeremiah 17:7–8. Make a specific list of what happens to the man (or woman) who trusts in the Lord. Again, drawing a visual aid will help you see the contrast between the two people described in Jeremiah 17:5–8.

8. While I was writing this chapter, Barbara often commented to me how upset she was that she had been set up as someone's idol. If you are the one who is discipling someone, how can you help her guard against letting you become her idol?

9

A Twist in the Journey

Let no one look down on your youthfulness, but rather in speech, conduct, love, faith and purity, show yourself an example of those who believe.
(1 Timothy 4:12)

• • • • • • • • • • • •

When Gina's children were in elementary school, she took them to a water park on a hot summer afternoon. The highlight of the park was a huge bucket, suspended high above the attendees. She has a picture of the children standing underneath that bucket, anticipating its tipping gallons of water onto them. She also snapped another picture after the bucket had deluged them. In the second picture, they are not in the same position as the first. The force of the water was so great that it had moved them out of their original positions. Thankfully, they managed to remain upright! Sometimes, situations in life can move us out of our "original positions" within our relationships, just as the water moved Gina's children under its force. Sometimes, too, we get knocked around a bit. Gina and I had a few of these "watershed" moments over the course of our relationship, when she became the one counseling rather than just the one needing discipling. While these times moved our roles around, they didn't knock us down; in fact, they served to strengthen our relationship along the journey.

When Roles Are Reversed

There were several events that helped Gina see that, although I was the "older woman," I, too, needed discipleship and counsel. One of those events happened over fifteen years ago. This incident occurred shortly after my husband and I realized that God would have us change churches after being members of our previous church for twenty-six years. Leaving a church is always difficult, but especially when you have known and loved people for such a long period of time. However, we knew that God was moving us to a different and new ministry.

This event involved my being "uninvited" to attend a ladies' retreat. This "uninvitation" was hurtful to say the least. Although my place of ministry was changing, my love for the ladies at the church never wavered. My goal in attending the ladies' retreat was to reaffirm my love for them.

When I received the first call from one of my dearest friends asking me not to attend, I was stunned and grieved. I burst into tears and called Gina. Through our talking together, she was able to comfort me. I was thankful that Gina was there for me and that I wasn't going through this difficult time alone. Rather, it was comforting to know that I had a kindred spirit with whom I could share this pain. Looking back on that time, I can see how Gina was fulfilling Romans 12:15 which says, "Rejoice with those who rejoice, and weep with those who weep." Gina wept with me.

I continued to receive painful phone calls from the same woman over the next few weeks. She couldn't give me a solid, biblical reason why my presence at the retreat was not desired. Instead, she told me that "time would heal" the broken relationships.[43] However, from my perspective, there was no cause or need for a break in the relationships. We were still sisters in Christ. I felt as if I was being punished by the ladies of the leadership team because God was taking my family to a new ministry. Needless to say, the ongoing phone conversations were very confusing and upsetting to me. I would immediately call Gina for counsel.

It was during this twist in our journey, or "watershed" event, that Gina was able to begin to counsel me. One of the first things Gina helped me see is that I did not have to sin in my response to the phone calls. She helped me remember to "sit down" in my heart rather than rise up in pride. She encouraged me to strive for a gentle and quiet spirit (1 Peter 3:4). She also helped me come up with questions to ask during the phone conversations rather than argue with this lady. Asking questions instead of articulating one's own position in a volatile situation is a better way to communicate. It also de-escalates a possible conflict. As Stuart Scott and others have taught, "Questions prick the conscience, but accusations

---

43 "Time will heal" is an unbiblical concept. Healing (reconciliation) comes when forgiveness is asked for and forgiveness is granted. When issues are not resolved quickly and time is allowed to lapse then several things happen. One, we tend to reinterpret the events. Two, we reinterpret the events in a way that favors ourselves (Prov. 16:2). Thirdly, bitterness is ripe for growth.

harden the heart!" These prepared questions helped me to better deal with the confusing phone conversations and to respond in a calm and gentle manner.

More importantly, Gina helped me put off the "fear of man" and put on the "fear of the Lord." I had a bad case of "fear of man" and had walked habitually in this manner for most of my life. Proverbs 29:25 says, "The fear of man brings a snare, But he who trusts in the LORD will be exalted." The fear of man is a biblical term for what is commonly called peer pressure, people-pleasing, codependency, or being shy and self-conscious. Bottom line, the fear of man is being controlled by the opinions of others. When we fear man, we become people pleasers who try to win the approval of others.

The fear of man can manifest itself in two extreme ways. One way the fear of man is demonstrated is through timidity. This person may cower when she is in the presence of others, particularly when she is first meeting someone. She may also hesitate to give her opinion on matters or to answer questions in a Bible study for fear of what others may think about her. At the opposite end, people are often boisterous and demand the constant attention and respect of others. This is another way that the fear of man is exhibited. Dr. Edward Welch puts it this way. "'Fear' in the biblical sense is a much broader word. It includes being afraid of someone, but it extends to holding someone in awe, being controlled or mastered by people, worshiping other people, putting your trust in people, or needing people."[44] Fear of man absolutely brings a snare!

"A snare is something that lures people away from their real purpose in order to destroy them."[45] In their book entitled *Courage*, Dr. Wayne Mack and Joshua Mack point out that a snare is deceptive, distracting, and destructive. Fear of man is deceptive in that it looks appealing to win the favor of man, but then you are in bondage to other people's opinions. Fear of man is destructive in that it can keep us busy trying to please other people instead of our Lord. Fear of man is destructive because it can keep us

44 Edward T. Welch, *When People Are Big And God Is Small* (Phillipsburg, NJ: P&R Publishing Company, 1997), 14.

45 Dr. Wayne A. Mack and Joshua Mack, *Courage: Fighting Fear With Fear* (Phillipsburg, NJ: P&R Publishing Company, 2002), 80.

indecisive and also keep us from doing the right and necessary thing.[46]

My fear of man rendered me a people pleaser. Through the multiple phone calls that I received concerning the "uninvitation" to the ladies' retreat, it was apparent that the ladies on the leadership team were mad at me and they definitely were not pleased with me. This awareness was devastating to me so I turned to Gina to help me put off the fear of man and put on the fear of the Lord. The fear of the Lord develops a proper fear, a sense of awe and adoration toward the Lord. A person who fears the Lord, fears displeasing Him. Second Corinthians 5:9 took on a new and real meaning for me. "Therefore we also have as our ambition, whether at home or absent, to be pleasing to Him." Once fearing the Lord became the ruling desire of my heart, I was able to overcome my concern over these women's opinions of me. Learning to fear the Lord kept me moving forward in my new ministry.

Amazingly, when one fears the Lord there is freedom. Moreover, it is easy to make decisions and know what the next faithful step should be. Proverbs 9:10 says, "The fear of the LORD is the beginning of wisdom, And the knowledge of the Holy One is understanding." This Proverb teaches us that there is a cause and effect. Fear of the Lord is the cause and wisdom is the effect.

> This kind of wisdom skillfully orders a person's life in accord with the disciplined application of God's Word to accomplish God's will for God's glory. It puts God's character on extraordinary display in the ordinary course of life. It allows wisdom's practitioners to skillfully relate to people and carry out one's life responsibilities . . . . This wisdom creates a unique quality of "kingdom culture" in a world that is fixated on human multiculturalism . . . . Thus, the wisest person alive knows, understands, and lives out the most about Scripture and God.[47]

During this painful time period with my previous church, I learned experientially what Os Guinness meant when he said that

---

46 Ibid., 73–83.
47 Richard Mayhue, *Practicing Proverbs* (Scotland: Christian Focus Publications, 2003), 43.

we "live before an audience of One."[48] Furthermore, it is through this incident that Gina realized that she was competent to counsel (Rom. 15:14). Also, she and Craig left our previous church to join Jack and me in our new ministry.

Another "watershed" moment in our relationship occurred when my father passed away. Gina had recently attended an ACBC (formerly NANC) conference in 2008. She went to a breakout session entitled "Developing a Proper Theology of Change through Loss" by Jim Halla. She wanted to gain wisdom on how to counsel others through the grief of losing a loved one. From this lecture, Gina was able to share much of what she learned with me when my father went to his heavenly home. For example, she learned that grief is not a multistage process or journey. Instead, grief is the human's emotional response to loss. Loss is part of living in a sinful fallen world and so is death. Romans 5:12 reminds us that it is "through one man sin entered into the world, and death through sin, and so death spread to all men, because all sinned."

Grieving will either be God-honoring or God-dishonoring. If we want to grieve in a way that honors God, then we should look to Christ as our example. Jesus' manner of grieving was uncomplicated, devoid of self-pity, doubts, bitterness, or resentment. Jesus did not have to go through multiple stages of grief or an arduous journey. Instead, His focus was "not on His loss but on what God was providing for Him and His people in the loss. The cross teaches, among other things, that loss rightly responded to will bring great benefit now and eternally."[49] Looking to the cross does not minimize your loss; it just maximizes God's grace. The cross shows how gain comes from loss.[50] The instruction Gina gained from this lecture was a big help to me in the loss of my father. It was another way God allowed her to become my counselor.

As I have shared briefly the two incidents that were "watershed" moments in our relationship, I want to leave you with a few warnings. There may come a time when the "older woman" may

48 Os Guinness, The Call: Finding and Fulfilling the Central Purpose of Your Life (Chicago, IL: Moody Press, 1992); quoted in Elyse Fitzpatrick, Idols of the Heart (Phillipsburg, NJ: P&R Publishing, 2001), 167.
49 Jim Halla, "Developing a Proper Theology of Change through Loss," A lecture given at an annual NANC (ACBC) Conference; October 8, 2008.
50 Ibid.

not want to listen to the "younger woman's" counsel. There have been many times when Gina and I have joked about how I "spurn" her counsel. One incident was when she was trying to help me see how I should respond to someone who had sinned against me. The Bible clearly says if someone sins against you then you are commanded to "go" (Matt. 18:15).

However, I had been hesitant to go to this particular person because I was trying to overlook a transgression (Prov. 19:11). Gina insisted that I should take her counsel because every time a new facet of the original problem surfaced, I struggled again, thus showing me that I was not overlooking this transgression. One of the times, according to Ken Sande, that you would not overlook an offense is when the offense has hindered your relationship. My relationship with this person had definitely been hindered; therefore, I was obligated to humble myself, listen to Gina, and go to this person.

There are a couple of things to learn from my "spurning" Gina's counsel. First, the younger women should not get discouraged and give up giving sound counsel to her older friend! In his instruction to Timothy, Paul wrote, "Let no one look down on your youthfulness, but rather in speech, conduct, love, faith and purity, show yourself an example of those who believe" (1 Tim. 4:12). One may be younger than the other, but if the younger is giving wise counsel then the older person should listen. No matter our age, we should welcome counsel about situations that come up.

Second, younger women need to realize that the results of their counsel are not dependent upon them. While we are responsible for the counsel we give, we cannot make someone else receive it. Younger women should not assume the role of the Holy Spirit in the older friend's life in their desire to help her. Moreover, younger women should not take it personally if their older friends reject their wise counsel.

As a way of encouragement to all the younger women, there were times while this situation was unfolding that I would tell Gina that she was right. Eventually, I did take Gina's counsel because I knew she was giving me God's counsel!

I hope in sharing these experiences that this will encourage those of you who are younger that you can contribute in a meaningful way to the relationship. For a long time, Gina felt as though she was the taker in the relationship. This is certainly not the case now, however. I am very thankful for the twist in our journey and for Gina's counsel which she freely gives to me now.

For Further Thought

....

1. In considering your close relationships, have there been any "watershed" moments? Were these times for the betterment or to the detriment of the relationship?

2. Consider Proverbs 29:25. Have you succumbed to the fear of man? Do other people's opinions of you control you? Are you a people pleaser? How does your fear of man manifest itself? How has the fear of man snared you?

3. Is it your desire to put off your fear of man by putting on the fear of the Lord? We strongly encourage you to study the following resources with a group of ladies: *Courage: Fighting Fear with Fear* by Dr. Wayne Mack and Joshua Mack and *When People are Big and God is Small* by Edward T. Welch.

4. Consider 2 Corinthians 5:9. Can you honestly say before the Lord that it is your ambition to be pleasing to Christ?

5. Have you experienced the freedom from living only before an Audience of One?

6. How has the instruction in this chapter challenged your understanding of grief? Since grief, as a multistage process, is such a pervasive, yet unbiblical teaching, are you willing to change your mind about it to line up with the Word of God? We recommend a small book by Howard A. Eyrich entitled *Grief: Learning To Live With Loss* and a book edited by Nancy Guthrie entitled *O Love That Will Not Let Me Go: Facing Death with Courageous Confidence in God*.

7. Going back to question 1, if the "watershed" moment in the relationship was a loss for you, how can you apply the instruction concerning grief? Consider the following questions to help you assess yourself: Are you grieving God's way, that is, in a way that honors God or dishonors Him? Is your grieving full of self-pity, doubts, bitterness, or resentment? Are you grieving with hope?

8. Apply the instruction on grief to any loss you have suffered: a loss of health, a loss of a loved one, a loss of a dream or position, etc.

9. To the younger women: are you confident enough in God's Word to start counseling an older woman? To the older women: are you willing to humble yourself to receive counsel from younger women?

10

Entrusting to Faithful Women along the Journey

The things which you have heard from me in the presence of many
witnesses, entrust these to faithful men who will be able to teach
others also.
(2 Timothy 2:2)

• • • • • • • • • • •

I, Barbara, loved participating in most sports in high school. I can't say that track was my favorite, but it helped me to keep in shape for my favorite sport: basketball. I wasn't too good in the long relays, but I did well in the fifty-yard dash because it did not require endurance. I don't remember much about the various track meets that I participated in. However, one particular meet is forever embedded in my memory. It was a relay race with four runners; we were required to pass the baton to our teammates. You can probably guess why I am able to remember this particular race. Yes, I dropped the baton when I tried to pass it to my fellow teammate. Needless to say, we did not win the race because we could not recover the lost time which resulted from dropping the baton.

Passing the Baton

What does running track have to do with discipleship? Simply put, I don't want to drop the baton! In other words, I don't want to fail to pass to others the truths that have been so faithfully taught to me. When writing his last letter to Timothy, Paul admonished him with these words: "The things which you have heard from me in the presence of many witnesses, entrust these to faithful men who will be able to teach others also" (2 Tim. 2:2).

I have had so many faithful Bible teachers through the years, from my first Bible teacher to my current pastor. I consider these pastor/teachers to be God's gifts to His church (Eph. 4:11–12). They have patiently instructed me and imparted to me glorious truths from God's Word. I don't want to merely enjoy these truths and then drop them like the baton. I want to entrust them to faithful women who will then be able to teach others.

Gina is only one of the many women whom I have had the wonderful privilege of discipling. I have also had ongoing opportunities to disciple others through teaching Bible studies over the years. My husband and I have lived in several different states. Whether we lived in Texas, Virginia, or Georgia, I have had the privilege of leading Bible studies. For example, just recently, I was teaching a group of ladies at my home church. We were studying the Gospel of Matthew. We were discussing the incident where a Pharisee came to Jesus and asked Him which commandment was the greatest. Jesus answered him and said, "You shall love the LORD your God with all your heart, and with all your soul, and with all your mind. This is the great and foremost commandment" (Matt. 22:37–38). Jesus went on to add, "The second is like it, 'You shall love your neighbor as yourself.' On these two commandments depend the whole Law and the Prophets" (22:39–40). Jesus laid out for this expert in the Law the two commandments that all the other commandments hang upon. I was teaching the ladies the correct interpretation of these verses because these verses have often been used to teach a very self-centered, unbiblical worldview.

Many teachers, authors, and pastors have misinterpreted these verses by saying that we cannot love others until we learn to love ourselves. One writer states this unbiblical concept this way: "Self-love is thus the prerequisite and the criterion for our conduct towards our neighbor . . . without self-love there can be no love for others . . . You cannot love neighbor, you cannot love God unless you first love yourself . . . "[51] This author further promotes this wrong interpretation by going on to state that these verses actually teach a "command to love yourself."[52] Upon careful observation of this text, one can clearly see that there are only two commandments: love God and love your neighbor. There is not a third command to love oneself. This wrong teaching encourages the sin of self-absorption and is in total opposition to Jesus' teaching that His disciples must deny themselves, not love themselves (Matt. 16:24).

When I was at The Master's University, this was one truth that

51   Walter Trobisch, *Love Yourself* (Downers Grove, IL: Inter-Varsity Press, 1976), 11.
52   Ibid., 11.

Dr. Wayne Mack stressed. I can hear him to this day: "We are to love God and love others. We are to serve God and serve others!" Dr. Mack was constantly encouraging us to be others-centered. This truth that had been entrusted to me I wanted to entrust to the ladies in my Bible study group. I taught this truth to them, but I didn't just stop there. I wanted more for them, as God does for us. I discipled them in such a way that I helped them with ideas to apply and implement this truth. This is what I mean by discipleship through teaching. It's not just disseminating doctrine. It is coming alongside women and giving them specific ways to implement that doctrine. In other words, it is helping ladies take their formal theology and make it their functional theology. When I teach, I make it a goal to plan the time to disciple in this way.

I noticed one lady in particular who was paying close attention as I was teaching through this passage. This concept seemed to be resounding in her soul. The next week, she came to me and said that she had walked around all week repeating, "I am here to love God and love others. I am here to serve God and serve others." This was particularly meaningful to me because in the weeks ahead she was able to minister to her husband with a sweet servant's attitude as he lay on his deathbed. This incident is a concrete example of how practical good theology is. This illustration is just one of many to show how we can take the biblical truths that others have entrusted to us and pass them on to others.

God has also given me opportunities to minister the Word through the counseling ministry at our church. Although discipling women in a group Bible study is a privilege, it is a particular joy to do "intentional" discipleship through counseling someone one-on-one. For instance, Jessica is a lady who had started coming to our church a few years ago. She requested formal counseling because her husband had left her for another woman. She was suffering intensely from her husband's sin. Jessica and I spent many hours together in the counseling room and on the phone. She submitted to God's Word and to the trial that God had providentially allowed her to undergo in a manner that honored God. I had to teach her much doctrine in order for her to endure this painful trial. We talked about the attributes of God (Deut. 7:9; Ps. 103:19; 119:68). We discussed a biblical theology of suffering (Ps. 119:67, 71, 75; James 1:1–8; 1 Peter 1:6–9). We also talked about what truly causes our behavior and the idols of the heart (Mark 7:18–23; Ezek. 14:1–8). I recently asked Jessica what biblical truth helped her the most. Her answer came as no surprise to me. She said, "There is no Plan B." She was referring to a theological truth that has helped so many who have suffered at the hands of others.

The truth Jessica was referring to has been explained in depth by better theologians than I am, but let me try to explain it in a nutshell. What I am talking about is how the two wills of God work together for one unified, sovereign purpose. Some theologians have referred to these two wills of God as "His will of decree and His will of command" or " God's sovereign will and God's moral will" or "God's decretive will and God's preceptive will" (there are also additional terms used). I prefer to use the terms God's decretive will and His preceptive will since my brain can latch onto those words. Part of this doctrine teaches that God takes the sins people commit against us (His preceptive will) and ordains them to His righteous purposes (His decretive will).[53]

No matter what terms you like to use in referring to this doctrine, the real point is how did this theology help Jessica? Jessica thought that since her husband had sinned against her, her two daughters, and God (her husband had broken God's preceptive will), that her life was now on "Plan B" (her husband had altered God's decretive will). Her conclusion was wrong. Jessica was encouraged to know that she was still on "Plan A" for her life (God's decretive will), although her husband had broken God's preceptive will. In other words, people can thwart God's precepts and commands by sinning, but they cannot thwart God's decrees. By comprehending this complicated doctrine, Jessica was enabled to move courageously forward, knowing that she had not missed God's best for her life and she was still on Plan A.[54]

Job 42:2 teaches us about God's decretive will. He states: "I know that You can do all things, And that no purpose of Yours can be thwarted." Daniel also teaches us that God does "according to

53 John Piper has written an article that can be found on www.DesiringGod.org entitled "Are There Two Wills in God?" In this article, he is referring to what theologians in the past have called God's two ways of "willing."

54 This concept is taught in a mini book written by James C. Petty, *Guidance: Have I Missed God's Best?* (Phillipsburg, NJ: P&R Publishing Company, 2003).

His will in the host of heaven And among the inhabitants of earth; And no one can ward off His hand Or say to Him, 'What have You done?'" (Dan. 4:35). People cannot break, thwart, or strike against God's decreed will even while they are breaking His precepts.

The life of Joseph also illustrates how the two wills of God work together. Joseph's brothers sinned against him by throwing him in a pit and then selling him into slavery. They broke God's preceptive will. However, God used their sin to accomplish His decretive will for Joseph. At the end of his life, after Joseph revealed the truth about who he was to his brothers, he said, "Do not be afraid, for am I in God's place? As for you, you meant evil against me, but God meant it for good in order to bring about this present result. . . ." (Gen. 50:19–20). In God's sovereign providence, He can use people who sin and break His preceptive will to accomplish His decretive will.[55]

However, the supreme example of this truth is found in the life of our Lord Jesus Christ. While ungodly men were breaking the sixth commandment, "You shall not murder" (Ex. 20:13), they were being used by God to accomplish His decretive will. Acts 2:23 says, "this Man [Jesus Christ], delivered over by the predetermined plan and foreknowledge of God, you nailed to a cross by the hands of godless men and put Him to death." While these godless men were committing the murder of an innocent man, God was accomplishing His decreed will of redemption.

It has been such joy to watch Jessica, in turn, entrust what I taught her to others who are suffering. I taught Jessica not only theological truths, but I also taught her some counseling strategies which helped her to implement the truths. One strategy came from a homework entitled, "The Hexagon: A Plan That Gives Hope In Every Trial."[56] The original illustration was taught to Gina in the form of a triangle in a workshop at the annual NANC (now ACBC) conference. When she taught it to me, the illustration had six points. So, I changed it from a triangle to a hexagon. Jessica taught her girls this illustration. Moreover, Jessica has been able to entrust this teaching to others who are suffering in a trial. The

---

55   Another excellent resource is Jerry Bridges, *Trusting God: Even When Life Hurts* (Colorado Springs, CO: NavPress, 2008). In particular, see chapter 2 through chapter 4, although we highly recommend the entire book.

56   See Appendix C: "Practical Help for Dealing with Trials."

baton has been passed!

Again, these are just a few examples of how I have been able to entrust not only doctrine but counseling strategies to other women besides Gina. Gina's and my discipleship relationship, of course, has been unique. Gina has enjoyed the biblical doctrines that I have passed on to her, and she is now doing a faithful job of entrusting them to other women. Now that I have passed the baton to Gina, she is in the process of passing the baton to other ladies concerning doctrine and counseling strategies.

Gina started entrusting to others what she had been taught when she began discipling Ann. At Grace Bible Church, Ann had requested discipleship from the leadership. Pastor David approached Gina, asking if she would "take on" Ann. She readily agreed. Gina led Ann through the book *Disciplines of Grace* by Jerry Bridges. As Ann and Gina met each week, they learned more about the gospel and how to "preach it to ourselves every day." They learned more about God's faithfulness in conforming them to His Son's image and their responsibility in progressive sanctification. They also shared concerns with each other, spending ample time in prayer for each other and their families. Ann and Gina continued to meet almost weekly for about five years. Most recently, they went through *Reaching the Ear of God* by Dr. Wayne Mack. Through this discipleship relationship, Ann and Gina have become really good friends. In fact, Ann came to every one of Gina's chemo treatments over the course of two and a half years except for one, when her mom was sick and Ann had to take her to a doctor's appointment. Additionally, Ann stayed with Gina in the hospital during Gina's transplant.

As Gina grew in her counseling skills and became certified with ACBC, she was also able to begin training others in their counseling skills. She has been able to entrust these skills to other women who desire to grow not only in their own walk with the Lord but also in intentionally discipling others. For example, she has a dear friend named Erin. Her relationship with Erin grew closer when Gina was diagnosed with cancer. Erin served Gina in myriad ways, from sitting with her through six-hour blood transfusions to taking her to have her hair cut before her first chemotherapy treatment. Erin expressed to Gina her desire to counsel, seeing the importance of it in the local body. When Gina took on a young girl and her mother, she asked if Erin wanted to sit in with her to learn the flow and sequence of counseling, or what Dr. Mack calls the Eight I's.[57] As Erin and Gina discussed the case and ways to handle the situation, their relationship grew with each other and with the Lord. They were able to talk freely with each other, not only about the case and how it should be handled but also about what they saw in each other, strengths and areas in which to grow. Gina observed that Erin does a fabulous job of bringing the gospel to bear on the counselee's problems. It was instructive to Gina and also encouraging to her to see God use Erin's giftedness in this way. They have been able to sharpen each other (Prov. 27: 17) and enjoy a close friendship. Erin and Gina pray regularly for each other and each other's families as they continue to encourage each other to serve in our local body. Erin even taught Bible study one summer so that Gina and I could take a sabbatical to write this book. Erin is now competent to counsel, doing so on her own and with her husband.

Gina is also entrusting what God has taught her to a special young lady, who happens also to be her daughter. Needless to say, this is a particularly enjoyable relationship for Gina. While no one is sure of the exact date, Lauren became a believer some time while her mother was going through chemo the first time around. Lauren explains her conversion in this way: finally deciding to stop trying to do life on her own terms. Instead, she decided to willingly submit to the Lordship of Jesus Christ. She is growing in her relationship with the Lord, which is a joy to watch. While Lauren is Gina's daughter, she is now also her sister in Christ. Lauren has always been discerning and mature. Now, it is a great joy to Gina to help her implement many of the truths she grew up hearing. For instance, Lauren is learning how to ask questions rather than answer a fool according to his folly (Prov. 26:4–5). In this way, she is actually helping her friends think about their biblical responsibilities as well as fulfilling her own. As Lauren and Gina talk about situations that arise with her friends, she is also learning not to have "big toes." They discuss how to handle times that she is sinned against but also times that she should

57   This process for counseling can be found in MacArthur et al, *Counseling: How to Counsel Biblically*. See chapters 8 through 14.

113

not be sensitive or self-focused. These opportunities are helping Lauren grow in her fear of the Lord and put off her fear of man.

Gina is so thankful that the Lord has given Lauren this information at this young age and is excited to see how she will be used by God as she transitions into adulthood. Through the relationship with her daughter that God has blessed her with, Gina was able to be a blessing to a young mother she was speaking with recently. This mother was lamenting that her four boys were not staying small but instead growing up. Using her current relationship with Lauren as an example, Gina told her that she will be able to enjoy her boys in new ways as they mature. In this way, Gina was able to encourage this young mom concerning her children.

Gina and I are continuing to pass the baton not only individually but also together. We both just recently took special note of a young mother of four children. Emily has attended our Bible studies at church for the past few years. She appears to love to study God's Word and is an inquisitive student. She is the one who asks the deeper questions. Often this is a sign that someone has the gift of teaching. The summer Erin taught Bible study, Erin, in turn, asked this young mother to fill in for her one week when she was on vacation. It was obvious to us that God has given Emily the gift of teaching. She has an ease in front of people, communicates well and clearly, and brings in good examples that amplify the material without distracting from it.

Gina and I were able to have lunch with Emily and share some of our recommendations to help her grow in her teaching skills. She is excited to keep growing. We were also able to give her some constructive criticism by telling her that it would be helpful for her to slow down in her delivery. Like Gina, Emily has a tendency to talk quickly. We all agreed that with many of the ladies in the group who are older, it takes some people longer to process information. We would all be better off if we slowed down to give people time to process the truths of God's Word. We also were reminded that some of the things taught may be new to some people. So, that is another reason to present information more slowly. It is a good reminder that we are not just disseminating facts, but ministering the Word with the goal of implementing what we are being taught. A slower delivery gives people time to process and think about how the instruction is applicable to their own lives in practical, real-life ways. Emily readily accepted our constructive criticism, a true sign of someone eager to learn and grow. Gina and I were saddened when Emily and her family recently moved to a different state. Nonetheless, we look forward to hearing how she uses her gift to serve the Lord in her new local body.

I have given many personal stories of women Gina and I have been privileged to teach and disciple. In giving these examples, we hope to encourage you to start passing the baton of God's truths to others on your journey. It would sadden Gina and me to think that any of us would be negligent and drop the baton. We would also like to encourage you to be intentional in handing the baton to others. Our great hope is this: What God has called us to do, He will enable us to do!

For Further Thought

1. Consider the teachers who have faithfully taught you from God's Word. Don't neglect to thank God for these gifted men and women.

2. Have there been times when you have dropped the baton by not passing on truths with which you were entrusted? Consider picking it up and intentionally passing it on.

3. Considering 2 Timothy 2:2, how are you being faithful to entrust the truths that others have taught you to faithful women?

4. List ways that you are loving God and loving others, serving God and serving others.

5. Although you may not be equipped or able to teach a formal Bible study, you are still called to disciple others. Whom are you discipling? How can you become more intentional in this discipleship relationship?

6. We rest assured that in the course of your lifetime, you have been sinned against by others. Study the life of Joseph in Genesis 37–50 and remind yourself that you are still on Plan A for your life.

7. We have purposely cited many resources in this chapter. Consider ordering at least one of them and going through the material with a friend.

11

Finishing the Journey Well Together

Therefore, since we have so great a cloud of witnesses
surrounding us, let us also lay aside every encumbrance and the
sin which so easily entangles us, and let us run with endurance
the race that is set before us, fixing our eyes on Jesus, the author
and perfecter of faith . . .
(Hebrews 12:1–2a)

• • • • • • • • • • • • •

As I mentioned in the previous chapter, I ran track in high school. I also mentioned that I liked the fifty-yard dash rather than the long relays because the dash did not require much endurance. However, the Christian life is not a fifty-yard dash. It is a marathon.

Finishing Strong

The Bible often refers to the Christian life as a race. Paul writes of the Christian's race in First Corinthians after he reminds the believers in Corinth that he does "all things for the sake of the gospel (1 Cor. 9:23). He then asks them, "Do you not know that those who run in a race all run, but only one receives the prize? Run in such a way that you may win" (v. 24). He continues by telling them what it will take to run well—self-control and discipline (vv. 25, 27). This self-control will include running in such a way, "as not without aim" (v. 26). In other words, we must be intentional and focused in how we run.

Hebrews 12:1–3 also tells us that we should run the Christian race in an intentional and focused way:

> Therefore, since we have so great a cloud of witnesses surrounding us, let us also lay aside every encumbrance and the sin which so easily entangles us, and let us run with endurance the race that is set before us, fixing our eyes on Jesus, the author and perfecter of faith, who for the joy set before Him endured the cross, despising the shame, and has sat down at the right hand of the throne of God. For consider

Him who has endured such hostility by sinners against Himself, so that you will not grow weary and lose heart.

When a runner runs, he intentionally lays aside anything that would weigh him down, any encumbrance that would slow his progress. He would not run carrying a backpack full of objects. He would not adorn himself with heavy clothing such as an overcoat and a wool hat. No, he would lay aside these encumbrances and run in appropriate running clothes and shoes.

An example of someone who did not lay aside encumbrances as he ran his Christian race was King Solomon. King Solomon had such an advantageous beginning. He was taught by his father, King David, the man after God's own heart (1 Sam. 13:14). Solomon was named Jedidiah because he was loved of the Lord (2 Sam. 12:24–25). God gave the throne of the Kingdom of Israel to Solomon (1 Kings 1:30). When God asked Solomon what he wanted Him to give him, Solomon asked that God would grant him "an understanding heart to judge Your people to discern between good and evil. . . ." (1 Kings 3:9). God was so pleased with Solomon's request that He gave him not only wisdom but also riches and honor (1 Kings 3:13).

Sadly, however, Solomon made some unwise decisions, decisions that would prove to bring sinful encumbrances into his life.

Women were a serious weakness of Solomon; not only did he make many political alliances through marriage, but he "loved many foreign women" (1 Kings 11:1) and he "held fast to these in love" (v. 2). God had warned that such marriages would lead to apostasy; the harem of Solomon held a collection of some 700 wives and 300 concubines; and "his wives turned away his heart after other gods; and his heart was not wholly true to the LORD his God" (v. 4, RSV). He built places of worship for false gods to satisfy his heathen wives. The Lord was angered at Solomon's failure to keep his explicit commands and announced to him the rift in the kingdom which would take place in the reign of his son.[58]

How sad to see someone who was entrusted with so much, who was blessed mightily by the Lord, fail to run with endurance.

58   Merrill C. Tenney, ed., *The Zondervan Pictorial Bible Dictionary* (Grand Rapids, MI: Zondervan Publishing House, 1967), 802.

Solomon did not finish his race well.

Demas is a New Testament example of one who did not finish his race well. Demas was among the "fellow workers" with Paul who sent greetings to Philemon (Philem. 24). He was also with Paul sending greetings to the church at Colossae (Col. 4:14). How is it then that during Paul's final imprisonment, one who seemed a close companion would desert him? It could be that Demas feared the type of persecution he was witnessing in his friend. After all, Paul was suffering greatly, being imprisoned under grim conditions by the Romans while facing sure execution. However, Paul gives us the briefest of explanations: Demas loved this present world (2 Tim. 4:10). Because Demas was fond of, loved dearly, was contented with and well pleased with the things of this world, he deserted Paul and went to Thessalonica. James tells us "friendship with the world is hostility toward God . . . . Therefore whoever wishes to be a friend of the world makes himself an enemy of God" (James 4:4). Demas turned his back on his friend because he was encumbered with his affections for the world. He did not heed the warning found in 1 John 2:15–17:

> Do not love the world nor the things in the world. If anyone loves the world, the love of the Father is not in him. For all that is in the world, the lust of the flesh and the lust of the eyes and the boastful pride of life, is not from the Father, but is from the world. The world is passing away, and also its lusts; but the one who does the will of God lives forever.

Having loved this present world, Demas was greatly obstructed and did not finish his race well.

Now, I trust that none of us has a harem to hinder our endurance like King Solomon. But are we in danger of being like Demas? Are we in danger of letting our hearts chase after the things of the world to the extent that pursuing Christ is crowded out? So, what are some of the things that can prevent a believer from running well and finishing well? Health could be a hindrance for some, particularly for those who have underlying illnesses or those who know people who do. Some spend excessive time working out or researching the latest medical breakthroughs, all with the intention that "it's not going to happen to me." Some chase after beauty, spending time and money to make themselves appear younger. While it is biblical to steward our bodies well, we must remember that our outer bodies are decaying (2 Cor. 4:16).[59] We are not saying medicine is wrong or working out is bad or make-up is a sin. Gina and I both benefit from all of these. What we are cautioning against is making these things the priority in our lives. Or, to put it another way, we are cautioning against working toward the wrong goal. If the goal of caring for our bodies is anything short of glorifying the Lord, we've got the wrong goal (1 Cor. 6:19–20). That's when these activities can begin to hinder us as we aim to finish well.

Other possible things that would not necessarily be sinful in and of themselves but could still hinder us from "running light" are material possessions. It's the attitude of "trying to keep up with the Jones" materially that we're talking about. All of our "stuff" needs maintenance and care. It demands our time and resources. If we had less, it would take less time and resources. Encumbrances could also be such things as overloading our schedules with activities. For instance, enjoyable hobbies can become hindrances because they captivate our attention and leave us less time to seek eternal things, the things above (Matt. 6:33).

In the passage in Hebrews mentioned earlier, believers are told to lay aside not only encumbrances, but also the sin which so easily entangles them. The writer of the book of Hebrews writes about sin, a singular sin. The inference from the context of these verses (it follows Chapter 11, which is often called "The Hall of Faith") is that the sin which so easily entangles us is the sin of unbelief. The writer has spent a long time talking about all the heroes of the faith who accomplished work for God "by faith." For example, "By faith Abel offered to God a better sacrifice than Cain" (Heb. 11:4); "By faith Enoch was taken up so that he would not see death" (11:5); "By faith Noah . . . in reverence prepared an ark for the salvation of his household" (11:7); "By faith Abraham, when he was called, obeyed by going out to a place which he was to receive for an inheritance; and he went out, not knowing

---

59 For a biblical view on stewardship of the body, see Robert D. Smith, M.D., *The Christian Counselor's Medical Desk Reference* (Stanley, NC: Timeless Texts, 2002).

where he was going" (11:8); and the list goes on. So, after listing all of these heroes who walked by faith, the writer encourages us to put off the sin of unbelief which so easily entangles.

After putting off the encumbrances and the sin of unbelief, we are told to run with endurance. We must stay the course and never give up. We must never quit running.

We must be focused as we run. We must be focused on Christ, pleasing Him and serving Him or else we will become weary and lose heart (Heb. 12:3). It will only be by gazing upon our great Savior that we will run our race well to the very end. This endurance will only occur because of our Lord Jesus Christ. In fact, it is because of the Person and work of our Savior that we can rest assured that we will persevere to the end of our race.

The doctrine of the perseverance of the saints is the doctrine that states that a true believer will not abandon her God but will persevere to the end. Wayne Grudem defines this doctrine to mean "that all those who are truly born again will be kept by God's power and will persevere as Christians until the end of their lives, and that only those who persevere until the end have been truly born again."[60] John 10:27-29 emphatically teaches, "My sheep hear My voice, and I know them, and they follow Me; and I give eternal life to them, and they will never perish; and no one will snatch them out of My hand. My Father, who has given them to Me, is greater than all; and no one is able to snatch them out of the Father's hand." How secure that position is!

This secure position is stated beautifully in Romans 8:28-30, which is often called the Golden Chain of Glory:

And we know that God causes all things to work together for good to those who love God, to those who are called according to His purpose. For those whom He foreknew, He also predestined to become conformed to the image of His Son, so that He would be the firstborn among many brethren; and these whom He predestined, He also called; and these whom He called, He also justified; and these whom He justified, He also glorified.

---

60 Grudem, *Systematic Theology*, 788.

Our salvation is secure from beginning to end. Those who are foreloved are predestined, and will be effectually called and justified, and eventually glorified. This chain of glory is guaranteed because we are "protected by the power of God" (1 Peter 1:5). One theologian has stated this doctrine of the perseverance of the saints as the preservation of the saints. In other words, believers persevere because God preserves them.

So, the question is not *will* we persevere. The question is how *well* will we persevere.

Paul is one who is an exemplary model to follow if we are to finish well. In his last letter, he told Timothy that the time of his departure had come. He wrote, "I have fought the good fight, I have finished the course, I have kept the faith; in the future there is laid up for me the crown of righteousness, which the Lord, the righteous Judge, will award to me on that day; and not only to me, but also to all who have loved His appearing" (2 Tim. 4:7–8). In these verses, Paul modeled for us his resolve to finish well despite his suffering. Indeed, he ran his race unencumbered. He finished the course when he was martyred in "late A.D. 66 or early 67. Tradition says he was beheaded on the Ostian Way."[61]

Stephen is another biblical example of one who finished well. If you remember, Stephen was described as "a man full of faith and of the Holy Spirit … full of grace and power [who] was performing great wonders and signs among the people" (Acts 6:5, 8). Certain men bore false witness against him, stirring up the people, elders, and scribes to bring him before the Council because "they were unable to cope with the wisdom and the Spirit with which [Stephen] was speaking" (vv. 9–12). Instead of softening his message, he began to recount God's dealings with Israel starting with Abraham (7:2). He ended with a firm rebuke:

> You men who are stiff-necked and uncircumcised in heart and ears are always resisting the Holy Spirit; you are doing just as your fathers did. Which one of the prophets did your fathers not persecute? They killed those who had previously announced the coming of the Righteous One, whose betrayers and murderers you have now become; you who received

---

61 Tenney, *Pictorial Bible Dictionary*, 631.

the law as ordained by angels, and yet did not keep it (Acts 7:51–53).

Of this sermon, Spurgeon says, Stephen "could not have delivered that searching address with greater fearlessness had he been assured that they would thank him for the operation; the fact that his death was certain had no other effect upon him than to make him yet more zealous."[62] In the face of supreme opposition and even death, Stephen did not shrink back. Rather, he was faithful to the end of his race like Paul.

While it is unlikely that we would be martyred at the end of our race like Paul or Stephen, our goal should still be the same: to finish well. One great benefit of the discipleship relationship Gina and I have described for you is that you would have someone who is committed to helping you finish well. So how do Gina and I help each other finish well? One way we do this is by encouraging each other to continue to stay in God's Word. In order to continue to run our race well, we cannot "rest on our laurels," so to speak, but must regularly renew our minds (Eph. 4:23). We are committed to letting our thinking be informed by God's Word. While we spend ample time preparing lessons for Bible study and agendas for counseling sessions, we make sure we are feeding our own souls on the riches of God's Word. Communing with God in His Word and through prayer is the only way to ensure that we continue to be fed. Gina and I hold each other accountable in this area. We continue to share what each is learning in her personal time with the Lord. And if there were to come a time when one could not read the Bible for herself, we trust the other would read aloud for her and with her.

Gina and I also intentionally provoke each other to persevere through difficulties great or small. One small example which became great in our thinking because of the closeness of our relationship occurred when Gina was unexpectedly asked to interview for a full-time job a few years ago. My initial response was one of sinful, selfish panic. While I knew the job would be a financial benefit to Gina's family, I was concerned that I was losing

---

62   David Guzik, "Study Guide for Acts 7" Blue Letter Bible. 21 Feb, 2017. Date Accessed October 2, 2020. https://www.blueletterbible.org/Comm/guzik_david/StudyGuide2017-Act/Act-7.cfm

my partner in ministry because Gina wouldn't be able to attend Bible study anymore. One of my concerns was that Gina would not be able to support me during the study. She would not be able to be the backup teacher for me, nor would we have the time to discuss the study as fully as we had enjoyed doing in the past. Eventually, Gina and I were able to have an honest conversation about the ways our relationship would change. Through this conversation, Gina was able to assure me that I would be able to teach and teach well without her at the Bible study. She told me that God would provide another "Gina" to help me, not of the same kind or to replace what Gina was to me but another helper for me. Through this conversation, I was provoked to persevere through a minor difficulty.

A more pressing and ongoing trial I am experiencing concerns my eyesight. After routine cataract surgery, I developed cystoid macula edema in the retina. This condition impairs my vision in my right eye. To help me persevere in this difficulty, Gina has provided practical help. She attends appointments with the retina specialist when I have to go. She offers to drive me home at night when I find it difficult to see. She also calls attention to times that I am not complaining, thus encouraging my further obedience in joyfully submitting to the trial God has sovereignly ordained. Lastly, and most importantly, Gina prays often that God would fully restore my eyesight. She is confident that despite this trial with my eyes, I will finish my race in a way that honors God by not complaining against His providence.

Another way Gina and I endure is that we help each other pay attention to our souls. Hebrews 4:1–3 warns us that if we do not pay close attention to the condition of our soul then it is easy to drift away if we "neglect so great a salvation." We tell each other if we are struggling with something. For instance, while she was homeschooling, Gina struggled with her son's resistance to and lack of zeal for learning. She is an educator and learner at heart, but her son dislikes academics. His attitude toward schooling often brought out both anger and despair in Gina's heart. I helped Gina think rightly about what was going on in her heart, shown by her responses to this difficult situation. I helped her remember that her son was not her "project," and that God had not yet finished writing his story. I also encouraged Gina to hope in God's recorded promises, not in what she desires for her son. Let me explain. Biblical hope is "not a hope-so, but a confident expectation based upon the recorded promises of the living Creator who sovereignly sustains and guides human affairs to the predetermined ends that He has foreordained."[63] Gina was trying to write the end of her son's story in her own mind. I prayed for her but also I rebuked her concerning her worry over her son's future. I rebuked her by asking her, "So, now, you are a prophet?" This question reminded her that she is not God. She is not the One who knows the beginning from the end. I reminded her that her job was to be faithful in her parenting. In these ways, I have helped Gina not drift away but endure by paying attention to her soul.

A final way that Gina and I continue to provoke each other to finish the race well is by reminding each other to live with a heavenly mindset. These reminders probably happen weekly as we converse with each other, not just during times of crisis such as a cancer diagnosis but regularly in everyday life. This pattern is arguably the most important practice we do to help each other endure. It keeps us focused on the goal. Reminding each other that our citizenship is in heaven helps us to keep intentionally laying aside worldly encumbrances (Phil. 3:20). Our heavenly citizenship also helps us to set our minds on the "things above, not on the things that are on earth" (Col. 3:2). A Kingdom mentality encourages us to submit to our King which affords us much contentment. A heavenly mindset reminds us to enjoy Christ more because He is enough. We remind each other that we are living for and waiting for a better country, a heavenly one not made by human hands. Hebrews 11:16 encourages us when we read, "But as it is, they desire a better country, that is, a heavenly one. Therefore God is not ashamed to be called their God; for He has prepared a city for them." When we long for and wait expectantly for our heavenly city, then our God is not ashamed to be called our God.

Gina and I pray that this chapter has exhorted you to finish your race well. We pray that we have given you ample reasons to

---

63   Adams, *A Theology of Christian Counseling*, 45.

fight the good fight and that we have provided practical examples to follow so that you will not hold on to any encumbrances that might hinder you from finishing your journey well.

For Further Thought
....

1. How intentional are you in your race? Read 1 Corinthians 9:24–27 and list the ways in which you are being intentional in running to win your race? In prayer? In reading the Word daily? In fellowship?

2. Hebrews 12:1–3 instructs us to lay aside encumbrances. What encumbrances do you need to put aside? How do you plan to put them aside? Write out this strategy.

3. Hebrews 12:1–3 also instructs us to lay aside the sin of unbelief. What are you doing to grow in your faith? Remember it is not so important to have great faith but to have faith in a great God. List ways you are growing in your knowledge of God.

4. How can you avoid becoming a Demas, loving this world?

5. Our sinful propensity is to love this present world as Demas did. How does the love of the world manifest itself specifically in your life? Are you too enamored with your health? Your beauty? Your friends? Your religious activities? Your . . .?

6. While God is holding on to you, what is your responsibility to hold on to Christ? How are you running hard after Christ?

7. What lady in your life can provoke you to finish well?

8. Look around to find an older lady who is finishing her race well. Set up a time to talk with her to find out what has helped her to persevere to the end.

9. Is there a woman you can help provoke to finish her race well?

10. We have stated four ways that we provoke each other to keep running the race in order to finish well. We mentioned continuing in God's Word, persevering in trials, paying close attention to our souls, and developing an eternal mindset. Pick one area in which you are lacking. Write five specific ways you can begin to grow in that area.

Epilogue: So What?

But prove yourselves doers of the word, and not merely hearers who delude themselves.
(James 1:22)

• • • • • • • • • • •

Our friend, Dr. Wayne Mack, has often commented, after hearing a good sermon, "So what? You have given me some sound teaching, but now I need to know how to apply it." We want to sum up our book with some thoughts to encourage you to implement the challenge we have presented. Proverbs 14:23 teaches us that "In all labor there is profit, But mere talk leads only to poverty." How many times have you read a good book and then laid it down and nothing in your life has changed? We would hate for this to happen to you again.

The purpose of this chapter is to leave you with some final exhortations. First, consider the urgency of Jesus' admonition to make disciples, not just to go and try to make friends. Don't settle for being part of a social club that is often labeled "church." The church should be a discipleship-making organism. We want to encourage you to make Jesus' last command in the Gospel of Matthew your first command. Then, as you are going through life, be about your Father's business and strive to make disciples. In this pursuit of discipleship, you will find a trustworthy, faithful friend.

Second, remember that, as in all of life, our ultimate goal is to exalt Christ. Indeed, we are to "proclaim the excellencies" of Christ (1 Peter 2:9). Likewise, any discipleship relationship should be about jointly proclaiming the excellencies of our Savior. Psalm 34:3 says, "O magnify the LORD with me, And let us exalt His name together." The glory of God should be our main concern in all of our relationships, but especially in a discipleship relationship.

Third, we urge you to seek the Lord in prayer. Pray that your goal would be to proclaim His excellencies and to glorify Him in all that you do, remembering that the highest form of worship is obedience. As Jesus Himself said, "If you love Me, you will keep My commandments" (John 14:15). It's interesting to note that Jesus preceded this statement with an exhortation to pray according to His will. He said, "Whatever you ask in My name, that will I do, so that the Father may be glorified in the Son. If you ask Me anything in My name, I will do it" (John 14:13–14). Since the "harvest is plentiful, but the workers are few" ... we encourage you to "beseech the Lord of the harvest to send out workers . . ." (Matt. 9:37–38).

Pray that you yourself would be one of those workers! Pray that God would send someone to you who needs discipling. Pray also that you would be harvested by a faithful worker! Ask God to give you someone to come alongside you in order to disciple you. Since the focus of this book has been discipleship, we exhort you to examine your obedience in this area. You can have full confidence that what God has called you to do, He will enable you to accomplish.

Our final exhortation to you is to get busy serving the Lord in your church. Why are we urging you to do this? The primary reason is that ". . . the whole Law is fulfilled in one word, in the statement, 'You shall love your neighbor as yourself'" (Gal. 5:14). Loving God and loving others, serving God and serving others is what believers are to make the focus of their lives. Another reason is that we believe that, as you are busy serving the Lord, you may potentially meet your "Barbara" or "Gina." It is through joint ministry that you will find ladies who are likeminded. We have seen this happen numerous times over the years. As we've said before, run hard after Christ and look to see who is running alongside you. As you are running with these disciples of Jesus Christ, as you are seeking to glorify God, as you are praying, and as you are co-laboring, you may just find a faithful friend. Grab her hand! Your journey toward biblical friendship is about to begin!

Appendix A
Salvation
Worksheets

Salvation Worksheets

....

Supplied Courtesy of Martha Peace

• • • • • • • • • • • • • • • • • • • •

*Therefore having been justified by faith, we have peace with God
through our Lord Jesus Christ, through whom also we have obtained
our introduction by faith into this grace in which we stand;
and we exult in hope of the glory of God.*

Romans 5:1–2

• • • • • • • • • • •

*Martha Peace gives her permission to copy these worksheets
and use them freely or they may be obtained at no cost from
marthapeacetew@blogspot.com.*

"Who Is Jesus Christ?"

The Bible tells us much about Jesus and who He is. Many of the claims were made by Jesus Himself and many were made by others about Him. Look up the following references and write down what these claims are. Before you begin your study, say a brief prayer to God and ask Him to show you if these things are true.

1. What does Jesus call Himself?

    A. John 4:25, 26
    B. John 8:28 and John 9:35–38
    C. Matthew 27:42, 43

"Son of God" and "Son of Man" are Old Testament expressions for the Messiah who was predicted to come. The Prophets in the Old Testament knew that this Messiah was God and that He was worthy of worship. See Daniel 7:13, 14.

2. What does Jesus claim about Himself?

    A. John 5:39
    B. John 6:51
    C. John 8:12
    D. John 8:58
    E. John 10:30 and 14:7–9

3. The Trinity is three Divine Persons (God the Father, God the Son, and God the Holy Spirit) who are the same in essence and nature yet with distinct personalities. When God the Son, Jesus, lived here on earth for thirty-three years, He subordinated himself to the will of God the Father. Why? See Philippians 2:5–8.

4. The Apostle Paul says in his letter to Titus that "God is our Savior" (Titus 1:3).

   A. Who does Paul then say our Savior is? (Titus 1:3, 4)
   B. What else does Paul say about Jesus? (Col. 1:15, 16)

5. Who did Peter say that Jesus was?

   A. Mark 8:27–29
   B. 2 Peter 1:1

6. Who did John the Baptist say that Jesus was?

   A. John 1:29 and 34

7. Who did the Apostle John say Jesus was?

   A. John 1:1,14
   B. Revelation 19:16

8. Who did God the Father say Jesus was?

   A. Matthew 3:17

9. Who has the authority to forgive sins?

   A. Luke 5:21
   B. Who forgave the paralytic's sins? (Luke 5:17–20)
   C. What did Jesus do to prove that He had authority to forgive sins? (Luke 5:21–24)

Summary:

• • • • • • • • • •

Jesus claimed to be God by saying He:

    A. was the "Son of God"
    B. was the "Son of Man"

    C. was the Savior (the Messiah)
    D. had authority to forgive sins

Jesus proved that He was God by:

    A. the works that He did (for example, creation)
    B. the miracles that He did
    C. His resurrection from the dead

The teaching of the Bible that Jesus is God is not something that we can explain by human logic. It is a supernatural truth which we believe because God's Spirit illumines the truth to us. Next week, we will study in detail what Jesus did on the cross.

What Jesus Did on the Cross

Just about everyone in America has heard of Jesus and knows that He died on the cross. However, they may have many misconceptions about the purpose of His death. So, this week's lesson is a study on "What Jesus Did on the Cross."

1. How was Jesus killed? (Matt. 27:35)

2. What did the sign over His head say? (Mark 15:26)

3. What did the people say who were making fun of Jesus? (Luke 23:35–37)

4. How did the soldiers decide to divide up Jesus' garments? (John 19:24)

5. Which four books in the Bible contain the story of Jesus' death on the cross?

6. Make a list of what Jesus said as He was on the cross:

    A. Luke 23:34
    B. Luke 23:42,43
    C. Luke 23:46
    D. John 19:25,26
    E. John 19:30
    F. Mark 15:37, 38

7. What was the *purpose* of Jesus' death?

    A. 1 Peter 2:24
    B. Hebrews 2:17 ("Propitiation" means to satisfy God's wrath.)
    C. Ephesians 1:7 ("In Him" refers back to Jesus Christ.)
    D. Romans 4:25 ("He" refers back to Jesus.)
    E. Romans 5:9

F. 1 Corinthians 15:3

Jesus told His disciples that the "Scriptures" (The Old Testament) were about Him (John 5:39). Indeed, there are many places in the Old Testament that foretell of the coming Messiah and what He will do for the people so that they can be reconciled to God. (Sin had put a barrier between people and God because God is holy.) Jesus' death on the cross was God's way of punishing sin so that God's sense of justice could be satisfied. In other words, Jesus was punished in our place.

One of the most detailed descriptions of how Jesus took our punishment is in Isaiah 53. This was written by Isaiah over 700 years before Jesus was born. God gave this information to Isaiah supernaturally and Isaiah doesn't call Jesus by His name but calls him the "Servant."

8. How was Jesus treated by men? (Isa. 53:3)

9. What did He "bear" for us? (Isa. 53:4)

10. What happened to Jesus because of our "transgressions" (our sins) and our "iniquities" (also means sins)? (Isa. 53:5)

11. Isaiah 53:5 says, "The chastening (punishment that we deserve) for our _____fell upon Him."

12. Isaiah 53:6 says, "But the LORD has caused the iniquity (sin) of us all to _____ _____ _____."

13. What kind of sacrificial offering was Jesus? (Isa. 53:10)

14. Where was Jesus' anguish? (Isa. 53:11)

15. What will He bear? (Isa. 53:11)

16. Isaiah 53:12: "Yet He Himself bore the _____."

17. What was God's motive for sending Jesus to die for our
    sins? (1 John 4:10)

Summary:

• • • • • • • • • •

Jesus died on the cross to take the punishment for our sins. He
died in our place. He paid the full penalty and then He said, "IT
IS FINISHED!"

What Does the Bible Teach about Sin?

Last week we studied Jesus' death on the cross and we learned that He died to take the punishment for our sin. Also, we learned that God was satisfied that sin had been sufficiently punished and that Jesus' resurrection from the dead is proof of that. Today, we are going to study about sin—who sinned first, why they did, and why and how we sin today. Some sins are very obvious—for example, murder. Some sins are obvious only to God. Regardless of which kind of sin we commit, all sin grieves God because He is perfectly pure and holy. Therefore, we need to understand just what sin is and how to properly deal with it.

1. The first created being to sin was an angel named Lucifer (later his name became Satan). His problem was pride. He wanted to be worshipped like God was worshipped by some of the other angels. Lucifer made a "power-play" in heaven and God cast Lucifer and all his followers out. What did Lucifer want? See Isaiah 14:1314. List the five "I will" statements of Lucifer:

    A.
    B.
    C.
    D.
    E.

2. Lucifer had a real problem with pride. He should have been grateful to worship and serve God. Instead, he wanted all the attention himself. What was the underlying reason that he thought he deserved that kind of attention? (Ezek. 28:17)

3. Lucifer was the first angel to sin and Adam and Eve were the first human beings to sin. When God created Adam and Eve, they were innocent and without sin. God put them in the Garden of Eden which had a perfect

environment and then God tested their devotion to Him and God told them they could eat fruit off any tree except one: "the tree of the knowledge of good and evil." God warned them that if they disobeyed, they would die.

A. Satan was not content to leave well enough alone. He decided to try to get Adam and Eve to follow him by disobeying God. He appeared to Eve in the form of a serpent. See Genesis 3:1.

   1 How is the serpent described?
   2 What did he ask Eve?

B. God told Eve if she ate from that tree she would die. What did Satan tell her would happen? (Gen. 3:4)

C. Whom did Satan tell Eve she would be "like" if she ate? (Gen. 3:5)

D. What did Eve decide to do? (Gen. 3:6)

E. Before they sinned, Adam and Eve were very comfortable around God and not afraid of Him. What was their response to God now? (Gen.3:10)

F. God confronted them with their sin. Whom did Adam blame? (Gen. 3:12)

G. Whom did Eve blame? (Gen. 3:13)

4. Because God is holy, He has to punish sin. He pronounced judgment right then on Satan, Eve, and Adam. What was one part of the punishment? (Gen. 3:19).

5. After Adam and Eve sinned, they knew sin in a personal, experiential way. It had become part of their natural nature and was then passed down to their children and their children's children, etc. Also, the consequences of sin were passed down.

A. Why did "death spread to all men"? (Rom. 5:12)

B. What is the "just" consequence of sin? (Rom. 6:23)

6. The Bible classifies sin by different terms such as transgression, iniquity, wickedness, evil, disobedience, and unbelief. Look up the following verses and list what the particular sin is:

   A. Romans 13:1
   B. 1 Corinthians 6:18
   C. Ephesians 4:25–29 (These sins are obvious sins.)
   D. Ephesians 4:31 (These sins may be obvious or may be "mental-attitude" sins. Mental-attitude sins are sins that we "think," which may or may not result in an additional, obvious sin.)
   E. Ephesians 5:18
   F. Philippians 4:6
   G. James 3:6
   H. James 4:17
   I. James 5:12

7. All sin, whether open or hidden, is seen and remembered by God. What does God judge? (Heb. 4:12)

8. Is there anything hidden from God? (Heb. 4:13)

9. God is holy. Therefore, He must punish sin. Man sins. Therefore, man is separated from God and the result is death. However, God loves man. So, He provided a way for man's sins to be punished and for man to be with Him for all eternity. The way that God provided is "Jesus' death on the cross bearing our punishment." How is it that we can know that we, personally, are in a right relationship with God? That *our* sins are taken care of? See Acts 16:31.

10. Oftentimes, people know about Jesus but they are still depending partly on themselves to be good enough to earn their way into heaven. If that's the case, then they are not really "believing" (trusting) in Jesus' death on the cross to be sufficient to save them. The Bible says

that Jesus saves us "not on the basis of deeds which we have done, but according to His mercy." (Titus 3:5) In addition to not trusting the Lord Jesus as their Savior, many people are like Satan in that they do not want God to rule over them. They want to control their own lives, so they do not trust Christ as their Lord. If that is true of you, "God is now declaring to men that all everywhere should repent, because He has fixed a day in which He will judge the world in righteousness through a Man [Jesus Christ] whom He has appointed, having furnished proof to all men by raising Him from the dead" (Acts 17:30–31). Romans 10:9 tells us "if you confess with your mouth Jesus as Lord, and believe in your heart that God raised Him from the dead, you shall be saved" (Rom. 10:9).

Assurance of Salvation

Many times when people are asked the question, "Do you know *for sure* that if you died you would go to heaven?" their answer is something like, "I'm not sure, but I hope so." Today, our lesson will focus on what the Bible teaches about "knowing for sure." Because this issue is a critical one, before you begin to answer the questions, say a short prayer and ask God to show you the truth of His Word.

1.   A person who is "saved" is going to heaven when he dies. What do you have to "do" to get "saved"?

    A.   See John 3:16.
    B.   See Romans 10:13.
    C.   See John 1:12.

2.   Read the following verses and make a chart. On the left side, list what "saves" you and on the right side, list what will *not* "save" you:

    A.   John 14:6
    B.   Ephesians 2:8,9
    C.   Acts 16:30,31
    D.   Ephesians 2:4,5
    E.   Colossians 1:13,14
    F.   Galatians 1:3,4
    G.   Titus 3:4–7

3.   People think about their salvation one of two ways:

    They must be good and do things to "earn" it,

    or

    Jesus did *all* the work necessary and they must put their faith or "trust" in Him (alone) to be their Savior.

Nowhere does the Bible say that a person is saved by what he does or how good he is! On the contrary, the Bible says that the only acceptable sacrifice or punishment for sins is Jesus' sacrifice on the cross. Why, then, do so many people think they must believe in Jesus *plus* "earn" their way into heaven? Because it is logical from a human perspective. But God says, "My ways are not your ways and my thoughts are higher than your thoughts." We're not holy so we do not think like God thinks. Because He's holy, *all* sin must be punished. It is not enough for us to have done more good things than bad. All the bad had to be dealt with and that's what Jesus declared when He said, "It is finished!"

A. Look up the following verses and write down what God wants you to know about "assurance of your salvation."

1. Romans 3:28
2. Romans 8:1
3. Romans 10:11
4. John 5:24
5. John 6:47
6. 1 Corinthians 3:15
7. 2 Corinthians 1:9–10
8. 1 John 5:11–13
9. 1 Peter 1:3–5
10. Titus 1:2

4. There are basically three reasons why people don't have the assurance of their salvation:

A. They didn't know what the Bible teaches, or . . .
B. They have never really *put their trust in Jesus as their Lord and Savior.* Jesus said, "But you do not believe, because you are not of My sheep. My sheep hear My voice, and I know them, and they follow me; and I give eternal life to them, and they shall *never* perish

and no one can snatch them out of My hand" (John 10:26–28, italics mine).

C. There is no evidence of salvation in their life such as a desire for God, a longing to please God, or obedience to Christ's commandments. "And by this we know that we have come to know Him, if we keep His commandments" (1 John 2:3).

Summary:

• • • • • • • • •

Salvation is a work of God not a work of man. So, if you are having doubts, ask God to grant you repentance from your sin and faith in His Son.

Appendix B
Relating to Other People Biblically

Relating to Other People Biblically

....

"One-Another Passages"

The Bible has a lot to say about how we should relate to one another. We often fall short in our relationships with other people because we are selfish. Study the following passages to draw out the principles that God wants you to apply in your relationships with others and note how you can implement these principles.

Bible Reference	God's Command	How I Can Implement It
John 13:34–35		
Romans 12:10		
Romans 12:16		
Romans 14:13		
Romans 14:19		
Romans 15:7		
Romans 15:14		
Galatians 5:13		
Galatians 5:26		
Ephesians 4:2		
Ephesians 4:25		
Ephesians 4:32		
Colossians 3:9		
Colossians 3:13		
Hebrews 10:24		
James 4:11		
James 5:16		
1 Peter 4:8–9		
1 Peter 5:5		

(Adapted from Dr. Wayne Mack)

Appendix C
Practical Help for Dealing with Trials

Practical Help for Dealing with Trials: A Plan that Gives Hope

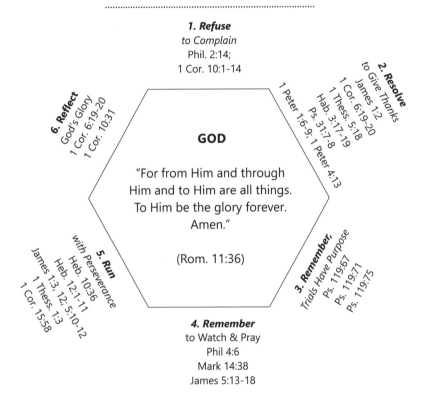

1. Refuse
to Complain
Phil. 2:14;
1 Cor. 10:1-14

2. Resolve
to Give Thanks
James 1:2
1 Cor. 6:19-20
1 Thess. 5:18
Hab. 3:17-19
Ps. 31:7-8
1 Peter 1:6-9; 1 Peter 4:13

6. Reflect
God's Glory
1 Cor. 6:19-20
1 Cor. 10:31

GOD

"For from Him and through Him and to Him are all things. To Him be the glory forever. Amen."

(Rom. 11:36)

3. Remember,
Trials Have Purpose
Ps. 119:67
Ps. 119:71
Ps. 119:75

5. Run
with perseverance
Heb. 10:36
Heb. 12:1-11
James 1:3, 12; 5:10-12
1 Thess. 1:3
1 Cor. 15:58

4. Remember
to Watch & Pray
Phil 4:6
Mark 14:38
James 5:13-18

*Know Your God: Your Joy is in Proportion to Your Trust
and Your Trust is in Proportion to Your Knowledge of God.*

1. God is Sovereign—Ps. 103:19; Dan. 4:35; Rom. 8:28

2. God is Good—Ps. 119:68

3. God is Wise—Prov. 3:5; "God always chooses the best goals and the best means to those goals."[64]

4. God is _____.

---

64 Grudem, *Systematic Theology*, 1257.

Practical Help for Dealing with Trials: Purposes of Trials

1. Trials come to strip us of self-confidence and increase our faith in God. Faith is the point, not our life (2 Cor. 1:9).

2. "For just as the sufferings of Christ are ours in abundance, so also our comfort . . . ." Trials are an opportunity to learn how to become better comforters (2 Cor. 1:3–10).

3. Trials teach us to value "things not seen" (spiritual, eternal) and not "things which we can see" (physical, temporal) (2 Cor. 4:16–18).

4. Trials are sovereignly ordained by God to test our faith and prove our faith to be genuine (1 Peter 1:7).

5. Trials—rightly submitted to—conform us into the image of Jesus Christ (Rom. 8:28–29).

6. Trials—rightly submitted to—produce endurance and maturity (James 1:2–4).

7. Trials—rightly submitted to—can elicit praise from the Lord (1 Peter 1:7; Matt. 5:12; Rom. 2:29).

8. Trials reveal what is in our hearts—what we love, serve, treasure, trust in—what we worship (Deut. 8:1–3).

Appendix D
Recommended
Resources

CHAPTER 1: THE JOURNEY BEGINS

Stephen Viars, *Putting Your Past In Its Place*. Eugene, OR: Harvest House Publishers, 2011.

CHAPTER 2: GINA JOINS THE JOURNEY

Donald Whitney, *Praying The Bible*. Wheaton, IL: Crossway Publishing Company, 2015.

Wayne A. Mack, *Reaching The Ear of God*. Phillipsburg, NJ: P&R Publishing Company, 2004.

CHAPTER 3: A CLEAR VIEW OF THE JOURNEY

Wayne Grudem, *Systematic Theology*. Grand Rapids, MI: Zondervan, 1994.

Ken Sande, *The Peacemaker*. Grand Rapids, MI: Baker Book House, 2004.

John Piper, *Don't Waste Your Cancer*. Wheaton, IL: Crossway, 2011.

CHAPTER 5: LOOKING FOR OTHER DISCIPLES TO JOIN THE JOURNEY

Martha Peace, *Damsels In Distress: Biblical Solutions for Problems Women Face*. Phillipsburg, NJ: P&R Publishing Company, 2006.

CHAPTER 7: SUSTAINED GROWTH FOR THE JOURNEY

John MacArthur and The Master's College Faculty, *Counseling: How to Counsel Biblically*. Nashville, TN: Thomas Nelson, Inc., 2005.

John MacArthur and Richard Mayhue, eds., *Biblical Doctrine*. Wheaton, IL: Crossway, 2017.

Wayne Grudem, *Systematic Theology*. Grand Rapids, MI: Zondervan, 1994.

Louis Berkhof, *Systematic Theology*. Carlisle, PA: The Banner Of Truth Trust, 2003.

Bruce Milne, *Know the Truth*. Downers Grove, IL: InterVarsity, 1982.

J. I. Packer, *Knowing God*. Downers Grove, IL: InterVarsity, 1973.

Arthur W. Pink, *The Attributes of God*. Grand Rapids, MI: Baker Book House, 1975.

A. W. Tozer, *The Knowledge of the Holy*. New York, NY: HarperCollins Publishers, 1961.

Paul David Tripp, *Instruments in the Redeemer's Hands: People in Need of Change Helping People in Need of Change*. Phillipsburg, NJ: P&R Publishing Company, 2002.

Elyse Fitzpatrick, ed., *Women Counseling Women: Biblical Answers to Life's Difficult Problems*. Eugene, OR: Harvest House Publishers, 2010.

CHAPTER 8: A NEEDFUL WARNING FOR THE JOURNEY

Martha Peace, *The Excellent Wife*. Bemidji, MN: Focus Publishing, Inc., 2005.

CHAPTER 9: A TWIST IN THE JOURNEY

Wayne A. Mack and Joshua Mack, *Courage: Fighting Fear with Fear*. Phillipsburg, NJ: P&R Publishing Company, 2014.

Edward T. Welch, *When People are Big and God is Small*. Phillipsburg, NJ: P&R Publishing Company, 1997.

Howard A. Eyrich, *Grief: Learning To Live With Loss*. Phillipsburg, NJ: P&R Publishing Company, 2010.

Nancy Guthrie, ed., *O Love That Will Not Let Me Go: Facing Death with Courageous Confidence in God*. Wheaton, IL: Crossway, 2011.

CHAPTER 10: ENTRUSTING TO FAITHFUL WOMEN ALONG THE JOURNEY

James C. Petty, *Guidance: Have I Missed God's Best?* Phillipsburg, NJ: P&R Publishing Company, 2003.

Jerry Bridges, *Trusting God: Even When Life Hurts*. Colorado Springs, CO: NavPress, 2008.

CHAPTER 11: FINISHING THE JOURNEY WELL TOGETHER

Robert D. Smith, M.D., *The Christian Counselor's Medical Desk Reference*. Stanley, NC: Timeless Texts, 2002.

Bible References in Each Chapter

CHAPTER 1
Proverbs 16:2
Isaiah 64:6
Jeremiah 32:38-40
Ezekiel 36:26-29
Matthew 4:19
John 8:32
John 14:6
Romans 3:10-12
Romans 3:23
Romans 5:8
Romans 6:3
Romans 6:6
Romans 8:28
Romans 8:37
2 Corinthians 5:17
2 Corinthians 5:20
Ephesians 2:8-9
Ephesians 4:1
Ephesians 4:15
Ephesians 4:22
Colossians 1:28-29
Colossians 3:9
Titus 2:3-5

CHAPTER 2
Judges 17:6
Job 42:2
Psalm 36:1
Proverbs 27:9b
Proverbs 29:20
Ecclesiastes 4:9-10
Isaiah 46:11
Jeremiah 31:34
Matthew 13:1-23
Matthew 27:51
John 15:5
Acts 16
Romans 8:16
1 Corinthians 10:13
2 Corinthians 5:21
Philippians 1:5
Philippians 2:2
Colossians 1:17
Hebrews 4:16
Hebrews 10:19-22a
James 5:16
1 John 5:14-15

CHAPTER 3
Psalm 119:59-60
Isaiah 43:7
Isaiah 43:25
Isaiah 66:2
Jeremiah 31:34
Micah 7:18-19
Matthew 6:33
Matthew 28:19-20
Mark 3:14

1 Corinthians 6:11
1 Corinthians 11:1
2 Corinthians 3:18
Ephesians 4:32
Philippians 2:1-2
1 Thessalonians 5:16-18
Hebrews 12:23
James 1:2
1 John 3:2
3 John 1:4

CHAPTER 4
Proverbs 3:5
Proverbs 16:9
Luke 9:23-24
Philippians 4:9
1 Thessalonians 5:14

CHAPTER 5
Deuteronomy 8:1-3
Proverbs 17:9b
Proverbs 20:19
Matthew 15:18-19
Mark 7:20-23
2 Corinthians 5:9
Ephesians 4:11-12
Philippians 1:27a
Philippians 1:27b
Philippians 2:3
James 3:13-17
1 Peter 2:9
1 John 1:9
1 John 3:7-8
Revelation 12:10

CHAPTER 6
Deuteronomy 29:29
Ecclesiastes 4:9-12
Isaiah 14:12-14
Ezekiel 14:1-8
Romans 8:1
Romans 12:15
Romans 15:14
1 Corinthians 3:6
1 Corinthians 10:13
1 Corinthians 13:7a
Ephesians 4:1
Ephesians 4:14-15
1 Thessalonians 5:18
2 Timothy 2:15
Hebrews 10:23-24
2 Peter 1:3

CHAPTER 7
Proverbs 27:5-6
Proverbs 29:11
Matthew 6
Matthew 6:19-24
John 3:16a
John 13:34-35

Acts 20:27
Romans 12:10
Romans 13:8-10
Ephesians 4:29
Philippians 2:3-4
1 Thessalonians 4:9
2 Timothy 4:3-4
Titus 2:4
Titus 3:15
Hebrews 5:12-13
Hebrews 10:24-25
1 Peter 4:8
2 Peter 1:3

CHAPTER 8
Exodus 20:3-4
Psalm 46:1
Psalm 115:3-8
Psalm 119:45
Proverbs 18:2
Isaiah 42:8
Jeremiah 17:5-6
Jeremiah 17:7-8
Ezekiel 14:1-8
Matthew 11:28-30
1 Corinthians 10:31
1 Corinthians 13:1
Galatians 5:22-23
Colossians 4:6
Hebrews 4:14-16

CHAPTER 9
Proverbs 9:10
Proverbs 19:11
Proverbs 29:25
Matthew 18:15
Romans 5:12
Romans 12:15
Romans 15:14
2 Corinthians 5:9
1 Timothy 4:12
1 Peter 3:4

CHAPTER 10
Genesis 37-50
Genesis 50:19-20
Exodus 20:13
Deuteronomy 7:9
Job 42:2
Psalm 103:19
Psalm 119:67
Psalm 119:68
Psalm 119:71
Psalm 119:75
Proverbs 26:4-5
Proverbs 27:17
Ezekiel 14:1-8
Daniel 4:35
Matthew 16:24
Matthew 22:37-38

Matthew 22:39-40
Mark 7:18-23
Acts 2:23
Ephesians 4:11-12
2 Timothy 2:2
James 1:1-8
1 Peter 1:6-9

CHAPTER 11
1 Samuel 13:14
2 Samuel 12:24-25
1 Kings 1:30
1 Kings 3:9
1 Kings 3:13
1 Kings 11:1
1 Kings 11:2
1 Kings 11:4
Matthew 6:33
John 10:27-29
Acts 6:5, 8
Acts 6:9-12
Acts 7:2
Acts 7:51-53
Romans 8:28-30
1 Corinthians 6:19-20
1 Corinthians 9:23
1 Corinthians 9:24-27
2 Corinthians 4:16
Ephesians 4:23
Philippians 3:20
Colossians 3:2
Colossians 4:14
2 Timothy 4:7-8
2 Timothy 4:10
Philemon 24
Hebrews 4:1-3
Hebrews 11
Hebrews 11:4
Hebrews 11:5
Hebrews 11:6
Hebrews 11:7
Hebrews 11:8
Hebrews 12:1-3
James 4:4
1 Peter 1:5
1 John 2:15-17

EPILOGUE
Psalm 34:3
Proverbs 14:23
Matthew 9:37-38
John 14:13-14
John 14:15
Galatians 5:14
James 1:22
1 Peter 2:9

They are gospel driven.
They are heart focused.
They are life changing.

Our Invitation to You

We passionately believe that what we are publishing can be of benefit to you, your family, your friends, and your work colleagues. So we are inviting you to join our online mailing list so that we may reach out to you with news about our latest and forthcoming publications, and with special offers.

Visit Us:

www.shepherdpress.com/newsletter
and provide your name and email address.